The Dhammapada

❖ Wisdom of the East Series ❖

The Dhammapada

Sayings of Buddha

Translated with notes by

Narada Thera

with a foreword by Bhikkhu Kassapa
and introduction by Dr. E.J. Thomas

Charles E. Tuttle Company, Inc.
Boston • Rutland, Vermont • Tokyo

✓

Published in the United States in 1993 by
Charles E. Tuttle Company, Inc. of
Rutland, Vermont & Tokyo, Japan, with editorial offices
at 77 Central Street, Boston, Massachusetts 02109.

Library of Congress Catalog Card Number 93-60005

ISBN 0 8048 1845 2

This is a facsimile edition of the work originally published in London by John Murray in 1954.

PRINTED IN THE UNITED STATES

The Gift of Truth excels all other gifts.

CONTENTS

		PAGE
	Foreword	vii
	Preface	ix
	Introduction	1
I	The Twin Verses	15
II	Heedfulness	19
III	The Mind	22
IV	Flowers	25
V	Fools	28
VI	The Wise	31
VII	The Arahat	34
VIII	Thousands	37
IX	Evil	40
X	Punishment, or the Rod	43
XI	Old Age	46
XII	The Self	48
XIII	The World	50
XIV	The Buddha	53
XV	Happiness	56
XVI	Affections	58
XVII	Anger	60
XVIII	Taints	62
XIX	The Just or the Righteous	65
XX	The Way	68
XXI	Miscellaneous	71
XXII	Hell	73
XXIII	The Elephant	75
XXIV	Craving	77
XXV	The Bhikkhu or Mendicant Monk	81
XXVI	The Brāhmana	84

EDITORIAL NOTE

WHEN the Wisdom of the East Series first appeared in the early part of this century, it introduced the rich heritage of Eastern thought to Western readers. Spanning time and place from ancient Egypt to Imperial Japan, it carries the words of Buddha, Confucius, Lao Tzu, Muhammad, and other great spiritual leaders. Today, in our time of increased tension between East and West, it is again important to publish these classics of Eastern philosophy, religion, and poetry. In doing so, we hope the Wisdom of the East Series will serve as a bridge of understanding between cultures, and continue to emulate the words of its founding editor, J. L. Cranmer-Byng:

> *[I] desire above all things that these books shall be the ambassadors of good-will between East and West, [and] hope that they will contribute to a fuller knowledge of the great cultural heritage of the East.*

FOREWORD

By BHIKKHU KASSAPA

If I were to name any book from the whole Tipiṭaka as having been of most service to me, I should without hesitation choose the *Dhammapada*. And it goes without saying that, to me, it is the best single book in all the wide world of literature. For forty years and more it has been my constant companion and never-failing solace in every kind of misfortune and grief.

There is not a trouble that man is heir to, for which the Lord over sorrow cannot point out cause and prescribe sure remedy. One never turns in vain to these stanzas of incomparable beauty for advice, for alleviation of life's manifold pains, or for message of cheer and penetrating insight. This is natural, since in the Arahat's words :

Lo ! now to us there cometh Gotama
In great compassion for us (all distressed) ;
Through word of him, who is beyond the gods ;
Nigh have we drawn to One who seeth, knoweth.

It is impossible to reproduce the terse elegance and glorious beauty of the original Pāli stanzas in a prose translation. The present work seeks mainly to offer a correct rendering of the Teacher's words as passed on to us through the Theras of yore. Each stanza was a " prescription " or part of one, designed to meet the complex needs of some person or event.

May this work bring to others the peace and the encouragement that the *Dhammapada* has so often given in many lands to generation after generation of its devotees, ever since its verses of crystallized wisdom flowed from the lips of the Lord of Boundless Compassion.

The present translation is by the esteemed *Thera* Nārada, a Sinhala, and a revered member of the ancient Holy Order of the Blessed One.

PREFACE

THE *Dhammapada* is one of the fifteen important treatises that comprise the *Khuddaka Nikāya*, the fifth Smaller Collection of the *Sutta Piṭaka*, the Basket of Discourses.

It was the Arahats who rehearsed the Word of the Buddha at the First Council held at Rājagaha, three months after the passing away of the Teacher, and who arranged and classified the book in its present form, naming it the *Dhammapada*.

Here the Pāli term *dhamma*, Sanskrit *dharma*, is used in the sense of Sayings or Teachings of the Buddha. *Pada* implies sections, portions, parts, or means way. *Dhammapada* may be rendered, 'Sections or Portions of the Dhamma', 'The Way of the Dhamma'. It is somewhat difficult to offer a graceful English equivalent according to its literal meaning. "The Way of Truth", "The Way of Righteousness", "The Path of Virtue", are terms that have been suggested by various scholars.

The *Dhammapada* consists of 423 melodious Pāli verses, uttered by the Buddha on about 300 occasions, to suit the temperaments of the listeners in the course of his preaching tours during his ministry of forty-five years. Circumstances that led to these noble utterances are presented in the form of short or long stories, together with traditional interpretations of the Pāli verses and technical terms, in the voluminous commentary written by Buddhaghosa. This valuable commentary has been ably translated by E. W. Burlinghame for the Harvard Oriental Series. It must be said that most of these verses are better understood when read with the context.

The gems of Truth embodied in these texts aptly illustrate the moral and philosophical teachings of Buddhism.

The very first two stanzas briefly represent the ethico-philosophical system of the Buddha. The importance of the mind in assessing morality, the Buddhist law of moral causation (*kamma*), the problem of pain and happiness, individual moral responsibility, etc., find expression in these twin verses. The third chapter is of special significance as it enables one to understand the Buddhist conception of mind. The first two chapters mainly deal with the ethics of Buddhism and are of equal importance to both bhikkhus and laymen. It was the first verse on " Heedfulness " in the second chapter that completely transformed the character of King Asoka the Righteous, who was originally stigmatized as Asoka the Wicked.

At times a single verse like the above, a solitary line like

> Seek no delight in worldly favours ; but cultivate seclusion,

or a pregnant word like " Strive ! " is alone sufficient for a whole lifetime.

The three verses, 183, 184, 185, which were originally recited by bhikkhus every fortnight in place of the present Pātimokkha [1] precepts, are very edifying, as they indicate the ideal life of a bhikkhu.

The chapters on Pleasures, Happiness, Hell, Evil, World, Flowers, the Fool, the Wise, Craving, etc., will prove very helpful to those who are engrossed in material pleasures. The illusive nature of worldly happiness and the kind of life one should lead in such a deluded world are shown in these chapters.

The chapters on the Buddha, the Arahat, the Brāhmaṇa, give much food for thought to the highly advanced.

One should not rest satisfied by a mere perusal of these golden sayings. They should be read, re-read, and pondered upon.

[1] The 227 fundamental precepts which every bhikkhu is required to observe.

Above all, these virtues should be put into actual practice. Then only may one rightly say, in the words of the *Dhammapada*, "Happily he lives who drinks the Dhamma".

Readers will observe the simplicity of the similes employed by the Buddha in the *Dhammapada*, which are intelligible even to a child. Take, for instance, the similes of the cart's wheel, man's shadow, the ill-thatched house, the sleeping village, etc. The greatness of the Buddha lies in his exposition of profound truths in plain terms.

Throughout the *Dhammapada* there is not a single verse that can be dismissed as unintelligible to a lay reader.

Direct teaching is the Buddha's usual method of exposition. At times he exercises his psychic powers, not miracles, in order to enlighten his deluded hearers or to give an actual demonstration to a concrete truth. See vv. 146, 147, 148.

To a fisherman named Ariya (noble), whom he saw fishing, the Buddha said, "Well, he is not an Ariya (noble) who is engaged in killing animals." The man realized his ignoble act and later became a Noble in the strictest sense of the term. See v. 270.

In the *Dhammapada* there are several instances to show that the Buddha not only preached to the intelligentsia and elderly folk, but also taught little children in their own language. See v. 131.

In preparing this translation I have consulted with profit the learned articles on the *Dhammapada* written by my revered teacher, the venerable P. Siri Vajirañāna Mahā Nāyaka Thera, the ancient Sinhala translation, and almost all the available English translations. Special care was taken not to deviate from the traditional commentarial interpretations.

It must be admitted that it is extremely difficult to retain the beauty and the spirit of the original Pāli in a translation like this.

In this third and revised edition, the first of which appeared in 1940, several improvements have been made, and copious notes have been added, mainly for the benefit of those who are not acquainted with the fundamentals of the Dhamma.

My grateful thanks are due to Bhikkhu Kassapa (formerly Dr. Cassius A. Pereira) and to Dr. E. J. Thomas for their valued suggestions.

I have also to thank Mr. J. L. Cranmer-Byng for having undertaken to publish this translation as a volume of the Wisdom of the East Series.

NĀRADA.

VAJIRARAMA,
COLOMBO.

INTRODUCTION

THE *Dhammapada*, the earliest portion of the Pāli Scriptures to become known in the West, gives us the " Words of the Truth ", that is, of the Dhamma.[1] The whole Doctrine taught by the All-Enlightened One. This is the sense in which the name is used in the work itself, where (v. 102) we are told how great is the value of " one single word of the Dhamma ". Further analysis of the meaning will be found in the Preface of the translator.

In one respect the *Dhammapada* differs greatly from most of the Master's utterances. It is not a continuous discourse, but consists of single verses or sometimes several combined, which have been uttered by the Master on the occasion of some special event during the forty-five years of his ministry.

We are fortunate in possessing a large commentary on the verses, which not only explains each verse grammatically, but also gives an account of the persons and circumstances that led to its utterance. The connection of the circumstances with the verses may often be only traditional, but the incidents have a quite independent value, as they frequently record events in the life of the Master, and also present some of the important principles of his teaching. They give us a picture of the daily life of the Master as it was understood in the early days of the community.

The verses which come first in importance are vv. 153, 154, the first words uttered by the Buddha on his attaining Enlightenment.

[1] i.e. Sanskrit *dharma* ; other technical terms in which the *Pāli* form differs slightly from the Sanskrit are *attā* (*ātmā*) " self ", *kamma* (*karma*) " action ", *Nibbāna* (*Nirvāṇa*).

No real story is given here, but we are told that the words were repeated at a later time to Ānanda, his favourite disciple and attendant, at Ānanda's request. After spending seven weeks at or near the Bodhi tree after his Enlightenment, he journeyed to Benares to find and convert his five disciples, who had deserted him when they thought that on his abandoning the wrong methods of meditation he had given up striving. On the way he was met by an ascetic, Upaka, who asked him who was his teacher. His reply (v. 353) was to declare his omniscience and his independence of any teacher.

Two of his earliest disciples were Sāriputta and Moggallāna. They were two Brahmin students, who had promised each other that whichever of them should first find " The Immortal ", the permanent state as opposed to the world of change, would tell the other. Sāriputta was the first to learn of it from Assaji, one of the five disciples. He revered Assaji so much that afterwards he would bow with clasped hands in the direction where he knew Assaji was living. The other monks thought that he was performing a heathen spell known as " worshipping the quarters ". They complained to the Master, but he, knowing Sāriputta's real intention, replied to them in the words of v. 392.

Some years after his Enlightenment the Buddha paid a visit to his native city, Kapilavatthu, where he converted many. The next day his father found him going from house to house for alms, and when his father protested that this was not the conduct for one born in the lineage of kings, his son pointed out that his true lineage was that of former Buddhas, who had gained their living in the same way, and he repeated vv. 168, 169. He also induced his half-brother Nanda to enter the Order. But Nanda was so infatuated by his bride that he wished to return to lay life. The Master then took him to the heaven of the thirty-three gods, and showed him the celestial nymphs, so superior to his own bride that he decided to stay in the Order in order to gain them, as the Master promised that he should. It was this state of mind that the Buddha described in v. 13. Nanda was afterwards completely converted, when v. 14 was uttered.

The Master's care for individuals is shown in several stories. For the sake of a weaver's daughter [2] he travelled thirty leagues in order to preach to her (v. 174), and on another occasion gave instruction to a farmer who had lost an ox (v. 203). The farmer was wearied in having had to seek his ox all day, and the Master took care that he should first receive some food. One of the most striking stories of this kind is that of the monk Tissa. In v. 41 is stated the hard truth of the fate of the body after death, but the story of Pūtigatta Tissa (Tissa the foul-limbed) throws a wonderful light on the character of the Master as a sympathetic teacher. Tissa was afflicted with a skin disease, which became so offensive that the monks put him outside and neglected him. The Master on finding out went and heated the water in the fire-room, and when it was hot was going to carry Tissa inside, but the monks insisted on doing so. He then caused Tissa's robes to be washed, bathed him himself, and when Tissa was again robed, with his body refreshed and his mind tranquil, then it was that the Master repeated the truth about the body :

> Before long, alas ! this body
> Will lie upon the ground,
> Cast aside, without consciousness,
> Even as a useless log.

The tale of Gotamī the lean (Kisā Gotamī) also refers to the inevitability of death. It is given here as an example of the style of the stories.

[2] See her story in *The Road to Nirvāṇa*, p. 40.

Gotamī gave birth to a son, but the child died as soon as he was able to walk. As she had not seen death before, she prevented those who were going to burn the body, saying, " I will ask for medicine for my child," and putting the dead body on her hip she went from house to house asking, "Do you know any medicine for my child ?" People said, " Are you mad that you go about asking for medicine for a dead child ? " She went on, thinking, " Surely I shall find someone who knows medicine for my child." Then a wise man saw her and thought, " This will be my daughter, who has lost her first-born son, and has never seen death before ; I certainly ought to help her." So he said, " Woman, I don't know the medicine, but I know one who does know." " Dear sir, who knows ?" " Woman, the Master knows, go and ask him." So she went to the Master, saluted him, and standing on one side asked, " They say you know of medicine for my child." " Yes, I know." " What must I get ? " " You must get just a pinch of mustard seed." " I will get it, reverend one, but in whose house must I get it ? " " In the house of one whose son or daughter or anyone else has not died before." So saying, " Good, reverend one," she saluted the Master, and taking the dead child on her hip she entered the village. Stopping at the door of the first house she said, " Is there any mustard seed in this house, they say it will be medicine for my child ? " " There is." " Then give me some." They brought some mustard seed and gave it to her, and when she asked, " Has no son or daughter died before in this house ? " they replied, " What are you saying, woman ? As for the living they are few, the dead are many." " Then take your mustard seed, that is no medicine for my child," and she gave it back. Going on in the way she had begun she went along asking. She did not get a mustard seed from even a single house, and in the evening she thought, " Alas, a heavy task ! I thought that only my child was dead," and then she perceived that in the whole village the dead are more than the living. As she thus thought, her heart which had been soft with love for her child became hardened. She laid her child down in a forest, went into the Master's presence, saluted him, and stood on one side. Then the Master said to her, " Did you get the pinch of mustard seed ? " " I did not, reverend one, for in the whole village the dead are more than the living." Then the Master said, " You imagined that only your child was dead, but it is the constant lot of creatures ; for the King of Death, like a great flood sweeping away all beings with their desires unfulfilled, hurls them into the ocean of painful existence," and teaching the doctrine he spoke this verse :

> The doting man, whose mind
> Is set on children and on herds,
> Death seizes and carries away,
> As a great flood a sleeping village. (v. 287)

As soon as the verse was ended, Kisā Gotamī was established in the Fruit of Entering the Stream, and many others also attained the Fruit of Entering the Stream and the other Fruits. She then asked the Master for admission to the Order. He sent her to the nuns and caused her to be admitted, and on being ordained she was known as the Therī Kisā Gotamī.

The commentary adds a later incident in her life, which illustrates v. 114.

One day, when it was her turn to light the lamp in the meeting hall, she sat down and looked at the flames dying out and springing up, and taking them as a subject of meditation she thought, " Even so is it with these living creatures, they rise up and pass away, and on attaining Nibbāna (extinguishment) they are no more known." The Master seated in the Perfumed Chamber sent out an image of himself, and as though seated face to face with her spoke and said, " Even so, Gotamī, these creatures like flames arise and pass away, and on attaining extinguishment (Nibbāna) they are no more known. Even so, life for a moment is better for one who sees Nibbāna than the life of those who live a hundred years without seeing Nibbāna." So saying he made the connection, and teaching the doctrine spoke this verse :

> Though one should live a hundred years,
> And should not see the Deathless State,
> Better is the life of a single day
> For him who sees the Deathless State.

Gotamī became known as "the chief of the nuns who wear rags", and it is of her that v. 395 was spoken.

The Deathless or Immortal State of Nibbāna is the state of the disciple at any time when full knowledge is attained. Then all his fetters and corruptions are extinguished. Hence the commentators speak of two attainings of Nibbāna. The latter attained at death is called Nibbāna without a remainder of substrate of rebirth. When the *Dhammapada* first came to be studied in the West there were scholars who declared Nibbāna to imply annihilation at death. Yet not only is there no such doctrine in all the Scriptures, but the view of a monk who appeared to hold it is decisively rejected.

In vv. 277–279 are taught the doctrines of the impermanence of all compound things, their painfulness (the first of the four Truths), and the doctrine of non-self (*anatta*). There is here no real narrative connected with the verses, but only incidents of the Master prescribing these subjects for meditation. The fact of the impermanence of all compound things was the truth realized by Sāriputta when he first heard the doctrine stated by Assaji. The term *anatta*, "selfless", has raised difficulties, because *attā*, "self" (Skt. *ātmā*), is used in two senses. When it is used of the self of actual experience it is never denied. In this sense it occurs over and over again in the Scriptures. This self (not the merely mental part but the whole individual) is analysed into five parts, the body, feeling, perception, the other mental and volitional activities known as the *sankhāras*, and consciousness. But the Jains and the Hindus held that besides these ever-changing elements there was something permanent, which transmigrates unchanged. It was this supposed unchanging reality behind everything transitory that is denied by the doctrine of non-self. The self as experienced is always changing, but the changes are continuous from birth to birth, and enough personal identity remains for one with the proper training to be able to remember his former lives. Rebirth indeed takes place under the form of rebirth-consciousness. This is no unchanging element, but only one form of the stream of being (*bhavanga*), which the individual assumes at the time of conception, and its further changes are enumerated in the twelve-fold Chain of Causation.

The Master's later life was disturbed by the intrigues of his cousin Devadatta, who had entered the Order. He was evidently an ambitious character, eager for gain and honour. Verses 9, 10 were spoken when he assumed a robe of which he was not worthy. He later proposed that the Master should retire and allow him (Devadatta) to lead the Order, but the proposal was rejected with disgust. Then he plotted with Prince Ajātasattu to kill the Buddha, but finally with the failure of all his devices, including the fomenting of a schism (v. 163) and his attempts to kill the Master (v. 162), he ended miserably, and at his death the Master (v. 17) spoke the words :

> Here he laments, hereafter he laments,
> In both states the evil-doer laments ;
> Thinking, evil have I done, thus he laments ;
> Still more he laments, when he has gone to a state of woe.

A long and complicated legend tells of the destruction of the Sakya clan, followed by the destruction of the destroyers. Thereupon the Master repeated v. 47, showing the vanity of human efforts overwhelmed like a flood by Death.

Other very different characters are the two chief disciples Sāriputta and Moggallāna, who both died before the Master. On one occasion Sāriputta was asked by the Master whether he believed that when the faculty of faith (*saddhā*) had been meditated on and practised much it is plunged in the Deathless, and finds its end in the Deathless, i.e. does such a one attain Nibbāna. He denied it, and the other monks thought that he was holding false views. But Sāriputta was distinguishing between *saddhā*, mere faith or confidence in the words of another, and *paññā*, the full knowledge gained by direct insight into the Truths. The verse (97) spoken on this occasion is a good example of an Indian riddle, depending on a series of puns, for it might mean :

> The man who is faithless, who is ungrateful,
> And has cut off alliances,
> Who has destroyed opportunities (for them),
> And is an eater of vomit, is a supreme man.

One without faith may be a misbeliever, but Sāriputta means one who has left mere faith behind and has reached full knowledge. *Akata-ññu* is " knowing the unmade ", i.e. Nibbāna, but if divided as *a-kataññu* it means " not grateful ".

The death of Moggallāna illustrates another important doctrine. The Jains hold that Nibbāna is attained when all kamma (the result of all deliberately willed action) is exhausted. But this is not the Buddhist view, for we find cases where disciples have attained enlightenment, but who are still suffering the fruits of their previous deeds. What is to be removed is not the kamma, but the evil tendencies in the individual that cause bad kamma. This is shown in the fate of Moggallāna, who in a previous life had been tempted to kill his parents. In verses 137–140 the Master explains to the monks the cause of Moggallāna's death at the hands of robbers.

One of the most attractive characters is Visākhā, the great lay-woman disciple. Her career shows the result of good kamma. A long story is told of her life and former lives. She was happily married and wealthy, but her father-in-law favoured the Naked Ascetics. They made charges against her and demanded that she should be expelled, but she successfully defended herself, and her father-in-law allowed her to stay. This she refused to do unless she should be allowed to serve the Buddhist monks. When she invited the Buddha with his attendant monks to a meal, she persuaded her father-in-law to listen to the preaching, and thus he was converted. She afterwards caused a dwelling for the monks to be erected, and bestowed many gifts in accordance with a wish that she had made in a former existence in the time of the Buddha Padumuttara. When the vihāra was completed she walked round it, and the monks thought that she was singing. The Master explained that she was repeating the earnest wish that she had made in a former life, and was rejoicing at seeing it at last fulfilled. She said :

When shall I give a fair palace
Plastered with cement and clay,
The donation of a vihāra ?
  My wish is fulfilled.

When shall I give couches and chairs
With bolsters and pillows,
With furnishing for beds ?
  My wish is fulfilled.

When shall I give the gift of food,
Food distributed by ticket,
With flavouring of pure meat ?
  My wish is fulfilled.

When shall I give the gift of robes
Of Benares cloth,
Of linen and cotton ?
  My wish is fulfilled.

When shall I give the gift of medicine,
Of ghee and butter and honey,
Of oil and molasses?
  My wish is fulfilled.

Then the Master, after recounting the former life of Visākhā in which she had made the wish, repeated the words (v. 53):

And as from a heap of flowers
One can make many a garland,
Even so one born as a mortal
Ought to do much good.

Several events of the Master's last years receive mention. The Sakyas, members of the Buddha's own clan, quarrelled with their neighbours the Koliyas about the use of the water of the river Rohinī. The Master went and dissuaded both clans from fighting, finally uttering the words of vv. 197–199.

There are two instances mentioned of calumnies, attempts by the heretics to discredit the Master morally. The heretics induced a wandering nun Sundarī to pretend to pay nightly visits to the Buddha. Then they caused her to be murdered and accused the Buddhists, but the murderers on getting drunk revealed the truth. Another wandering nun was Cincā, who made similar charges, and it required the help of the god Sakka to discover the truth. In both cases the words of the Master condemn the vice of lying (vv. 306, 176).

One of the most striking events both as showing the Master's method of teaching as well as emphasizing his fundamental principles is the conversion of Subhadda. He was an aged wanderer who came, when the Master lay on his death-bed, to have certain questions solved that were being discussed in other schools. The reply of the Master was to put aside all these questions and to point out what are the only things essential for a true ascetic. All that matters for the Buddhist is that the true ascetic must hold and realize the four Noble Truths and follow the Eightfold Path (vv. 254, 255). Subhadda then became the last disciple to be admitted by the Lord to the ordination of a monk (*bhikkhu*).

These four Truths (pain or sorrow, its origin, its cessation, and the Noble Eightfold Path) were set forth by the Master on another occasion, when he was discussing various paths along which the monks had been travelling (vv. 273–276).

The *āsavas* : this is a term sometimes translated " corruptions " or " depravities ", but this gives no idea as to what quality or feature of the individual is meant. As, however, they are described in detail, we know exactly what they mean. They are the three (or four) inherent tendencies in the individual which must be eradicated in order to attain the full knowledge of an arahat, namely, sensual desire (*kāma*), desire for becoming in any form of sensitive existence (*bhava*), and ignorance (*avijjā*) to which, as a form of ignorance, is added false view (*micchādiṭṭhi*).

Many other points of doctrine are discussed in the learned notes of the translator that accompany this edition.

DHAMMAPADA

HOMAGE TO THE BLESSED ONE,
THE ARAHAT, THE FULLY ENLIGHTENED

I. *YAMAKAVAGGA.*[1] *THE TWIN VERSES*

1. Mind foreruns (all evil) conditions, mind is chief, mind-made are they; if one speaks or acts with wicked mind, because of that, pain pursues him, even as the wheel follows the hoof of the draught-ox.

2. Mind foreruns (all good) conditions, mind is chief, mind-made are they; if one speaks or acts with pure mind, because of that, happiness follows him, even as the shadow that never leaves.

3. "He abused me, he beat me, he defeated me, he robbed me," the hatred of those who harbour such thoughts is not appeased.[2]

4. "He abused me, he beat me, he defeated me, he robbed me," the hatred of those who do not harbour such thoughts is appeased.

5. Hatreds never cease by hatred in this world; by love alone they cease. This is an ancient law.[3]

[1] *Yamaka* means a pair. This chapter is so called because it consists of ten pairs of parallel verses.

[2] Verses 3, 4 were uttered by the Buddha on two different occasions to show the inevitable effects of evil and good *kamma* (deeds) respectively. Strictly speaking, *kamma* is purely mental, and its effect is also mental. Where there is no mind or consciousness there is no *kamma*.

Mind precedes all deeds, and acts as the principal element both in performing and assessing deeds. It is mind that rules and shapes action. Physical and verbal deeds too are produced by mind.

In these verses the Buddha first emphasizes the great part the mind plays in man's life, and then explains how deeds become good or evil according to the pure or impure state of the mind. Lastly he speaks of the inevitable consequences of such deeds with two homely illustrations.

[3] An ancient principle followed by the Buddhas and disciples. (Cy.)

6. The others [4] know not that in this quarrel we perish [5]; those of them who realize it have their quarrels calmed thereby.[6]

7. Whoever lives contemplating pleasant things,[7] with senses unrestrained, in food immoderate, indolent, inactive, him verily Māra [8] overthrows, as wind a weak tree.

8. Whoever lives contemplating unpleasant things,[9] with senses well-restrained, in food moderate, replete with confidence [10] and sustained effort, him Māra overthrows not, as wind a rocky mountain.[11]

9. Whoever, unstainless,[12] without self-control and truthfulness, should don the yellow robe, is not worthy of it.

10. He who has vomited all impurities, in morals is well-

[4] The quarrelsome persons.

[5] *Yamāmase*, derived from *yam*, to perish or to restrain.

Another rendering: "Others do not know that here we must restrain ourselves."

"The world does not know that we must all come to an end here." Max Müller.

"People do not discern that here we straightened are in life, in time." Mrs. Rhys Davids.

[6] This verse was uttered by the Buddha in connection with a dispute that arose between two parties of bhikkhus.

[7] 'Looking for pleasures.'

[8] The term *Māra* is used in the sense of passions.

[9] Such as the thirty-two parts of the body.

[10] *Saddhā*, trustful confidence based on knowledge.

[11] These two verses are meant exclusively for bhikkhus. The first verse indicates the wrong path of sense gratification, the second the right path of sense-control and strict asceticism.

[12] Free from the stains of lust *anikkasāva*; *kāsāva* means a dyed robe, the symbol of asceticism. Here is a play on words. External mark of the holy life is of no consequence without internal purity. On another occasion the Buddha has said that a pure person is indeed an ideal recluse, irrespective of his external apparel. See v. 142.

established and endowed with self-control and truthfulness, is indeed worthy of the yellow robe.

11. In the unreal[13] they imagine the real, in the real they see the unreal; they who feed on wrong thoughts[14] never achieve the real.

12. Seeing the real as real, the unreal as unreal, they who feed on right thoughts[15] achieve the real.

13. Even as rain penetrates an ill-thatched house, so does lust penetrate an undeveloped mind.

14. Even as rain does not penetrate a well-thatched house, so does lust not penetrate a well-developed[16] mind.

15. Here he grieves,[17] hereafter he grieves[18]; in both states the evil-doer grieves; he grieves, he perishes, seeing his own impure deed.

16. Here he rejoices, hereafter he rejoices; in both states the well-doer rejoices; he rejoices, exceedingly rejoices, seeing the purity of his own deeds.

17. Here he laments, hereafter he laments; in both states the evil-doer laments; thinking, "evil have I done", thus he

[13] *Sāra* means the core or essence, *asāra* are the unessentials like the necessaries of life, false beliefs, etc. *Sāra* are the essentials like right beliefs, etc. The essence of the holy life cannot be achieved by caring for the unessentials.

[14] Such as lust (*kāma*), ill-will (*vyāpāda*), and harmfulness (*vihiṃsā*).

[15] Such as renunciation or non-attachment (*nekkhamma*), loving-kindness (*avyāpāda*) and harmlessness (*avihiṃsā*).

Pure thoughts lead to right understanding.

[16] *Bhāvitaṃ*, lit., made to become, i.e. trained, cultivated, developed. Mind is trained by concentration and contemplation. As physical exercise to the body, so is meditation to the mind. A fully trained mind is not dominated by passions.

[17] Repenting over his evil deeds.

[18] Experiencing the effects of his evil actions.

laments. Furthermore he laments, having gone to a state of woe.[19]

18. Here he is happy, hereafter he is happy ; in both states the well-doer is happy. Thinking, " good have I done ", thus he is happy. Furthermore is he happy, having gone to a state of bliss.[19]

19. Though much he recites the Sacred texts,[20] but acts not accordingly, that heedless man is like a cow-herd who counts others' kine ; he has no share in the blessings of a recluse.[21]

20. Though little he recites the Sacred texts, but acts in accordance with the teaching, forsaking lust, hatred, and ignorance, truly knowing, with mind well freed, clinging for naught here and hereafter, he shares in the blessings of a recluse.[22]

[19] *Duggati* is evil state, and *Sugati* is good state. According to Buddhism there are many other habitable planes besides the earth, but no state, with the only exception of Nibbāna, is eternal.

[20] *Sahitaṃ* is a synonym for the Tipiṭaka, the Teachings of the Buddha (Cy.) ; that which is associated with what is beneficial is *sahitaṃ*.

[21] Namely, the four stages of saintship.

[22] There were two bhikkhus, one of whom was versed in the Dhamma but did not practise what he knew, the other knew little of the Dhamma, but having practised what little he knew, he enjoyed the fruits of the holy life. The Buddha uttered these two verses in connection with them.

Additional note on v. 1 :

Here *dhammā* = *kamma* or *karma*, a many-meaninged term, which in this context stands for volition (*cetanā*) and the other thought factors that constitute any particular volitional thought-stream. Briefly *kamma* = action here (in thought, word, and deed) and its inevitable reaction.

II. APPAMĀDAVAGGA. HEEDFULNESS

21. Heedfulness [1] is the path to the deathless [2]; heedlessness is the path to death. The heedful do not die [3]; the heedless are like unto the dead.

22. Distinctly understanding this difference,[4] the wise in heedfulness rejoice in heedfulness, delighting in the realm of the Ariyas.[5]

23. The constantly meditative,[6] the ever earnestly striving ones realize the bond-free,[7] supreme Nibbāna.[8]

24. The good fame of him who is energetic, mindful, pure

[1] *Appamāda*, literally means non-infatuation, i.e. ever-present mindfulness or watchfulness in doing good.

[2] *Amata* = Nibbāna, the ultimate goal of Buddhists. Note the positive term used in connection with Nibbāna, which is not annihilation as some are apt to believe. It is the permanent, immortal state.

[3] This should not be understood to mean that they are immortal. All beings are mortal. The idea implied herein is that the heedful, who realize Nibbāna, are not born again and again, and so do not die. The heedless are regarded as dead because they are not intent on doing good, and are subject to repeated births and deaths.

[4] The fact that there is an escape for the heedful, but not for the heedless.

[5] Here Ariyas means the pure ones like the Buddhas and Arahats; by the realm of the Ariyas is meant the thirty-seven Factors of Enlightenment and the nine Supramundane States. See notes on v. 44 and v. 115.

[6] Here meditation includes both concentration (*samatha*) and contemplation or insight (*vipassanā*).

[7] *Yogakkhema*, free from the four bonds of craving (*kāma*), existence (*bhava*), false views (*diṭṭhi*), and ignorance (*avijjā*).

[8] *Nibbāna* = *ni- vāna*, lit., departure from craving. It is a supramundane state that can be attained in this life. It is also explained as extinction of passions, but not a state of nothingness. It is an eternal state of bliss that results from the complete eradication of the passions.

in deed, considerate, self-controlled, right-living, and heedful steadily increases.

25. By sustained effort, earnestness, discipline, and self-control let the wise man make for himself an island [9] which no flood overwhelms.

26. The ignorant, foolish folk indulge in heedlessness; the wise man guards earnestness as the greatest treasure.

27. Indulge not in heedlessness, have no intimacy with sensuous delights; for the earnest, meditative person obtains abundant bliss.

28. When the sagacious one discards heedlessness by heedfulness, this sorrowless wise one [10] ascends the palace of wisdom and surveys the ignorant sorrowing folk as one standing on a mountain the groundlings.

29. Heedful amongst the heedless, wide awake amongst the slumbering, the wise man advances like a swift horse, leaving a weak jade behind.

30. By earnestness Maghavā [11] rose to the lordship of the gods.[12] Earnestness is ever praised; carelessness is ever despised.

[9] An island situated on a higher elevation cannot be flooded although the surrounding low-lying land may be inundated. Such an island becomes a refuge to all. In the same way the wise man who develops insight should make an island of himself by attaining Arahatship, so that he may not be drowned by the floods of sensual pleasures, false beliefs, becoming and ignorance.

[10] The Arahats who have no sorrow survey with their divine eye the ignorant folk who, being subject to repeated births, are not free from sorrow.

[11] *Maghavā* is another name of Sakka, the king of the gods. The *Magha-mānavaka Jātaka* relates that in the remote past a certain public-spirited person, who spent his whole lifetime in welfare work, was born as Sakka.

[12] A class of beings with subtle physical bodies invisible to the physical eye.

31. The bhikkhu[13] who delights in earnestness, and looks with fear on negligence, advances like fire, burning all fetters,[14] great and small.

32. The bhikkhu who delights in earnestness, and looks with fear on negligence, is not liable to fall[15]; he is in the presence of Nibbāna.

[13] An ordained disciple of the Buddha is called a bhikkhu, lit. a mendicant monk. A bhikkhu is not a priest as he is no mediator between God and man.

[14] *Saṃyojana*, lit., that which yokes beings to the ocean of life. There are ten kinds of fetters, viz. self-illusion (*sakkāya-diṭṭhi*), doubts (*diṭṭhi*), indulgence in mere rites and ceremonies (*sīlabbata-parāmāsa*), sense-desires (*kāmarāga*), hatred (*paṭigha*), attachment to the Realms of Form (*rūparāga*), attachment to the Formless Realms (*arūparāga*), conceit (*māna*) and ignorance (*avijjā*).

The first five are regarded as small, the rest as great.

[15] From his spiritual heights which he has attained.

III. CITTAVAGGA. THE MIND[1]

33. The flickering, fickle mind, difficult to guard, difficult to control, the wise person straightens, as a fletcher an arrow.

34. Like a fish that is drawn from its watery abode and thrown upon land, even so does this mind flutter, so should the realm of the passions be shunned.[2]

35. The mind is hard to check, swift, flits wherever it lists, the control of which is good ; a controlled mind is conducive to happiness.

36. The mind is very hard to perceive, extremely subtle, flits wherever it lists ; let the wise person guard it ; a guarded mind is conducive to happiness.

37. Faring far, wandering alone,[3] bodiless,[4] lying in the cave [5] is the mind ; those who subdue it are freed from the bond of Māra.

[1] *Citta* is derived from the root *citi*, to think. The traditional interpretation of the term is that which is aware of an object (*cinteti* = *vijānāti*). Actually it is not that which thinks of an object as the term implies. If it could be said ' it thinks ' as one says in English ' it rains ', it would be more in consonance with the Buddha's teaching. From an ultimate point of view *citta* may be defined as the awareness of an object, since Buddhism denies a subjective agent like a soul, as understood by the Hindus. According to Buddhism no distinction is made between mind and consciousness, terms which are used as equivalents for *citta*.

[2] *Pahātave* is used in the sense of *pahātabba*.

[3] Because no two thoughts arise at one moment.

[4] Since the mind is formless and colourless.

[5] *Guhāsayaṃ*, i.e. the seat of consciousness.

It is clear that the Buddha had not definitely assigned a specific basis for consciousness as he had done with the other senses. It was the cardiac theory (the theory that the heart is the seat of the soul) *yaṃ rūpaṃ*, which prevailed in his time, and this was evidently supported by the Upanishads.

38. He whose mind is not steadfast, he who knows not the true Doctrine, he whose confidence wavers—the wisdom of such a one will never be perfect.

39. He whose mind is not wetted (by lust), he who is not affected (by hatred), he who has discarded both good and evil [6]—for such a vigilant one [7] there is no fear.

40. Realizing that this body is (as fragile) as a jar, establishing his mind (as firm) as a (fortified) city, he should attack Māra [8] with the weapon of wisdom; he should guard his conquest,[9] and be without attachment.[10]

The Buddha could have adopted this popular theory, but he did not commit himself. In the *Paṭṭhāna*, the Book of Relations, the Buddha refers to the basis of consciousness in such indirect terms as *yaṃ rūpaṃ nissāya*, depending on that material thing. What that material thing was the Buddha did not positively assert. According to the views of commentators like Buddhaghosa and Anuruddha the seat of consciousness is the heart (*hadayavatthu*). One wonders whether one is justified in presenting the cardiac theory as Buddhistic when the Buddha himself neither rejected nor accepted this popular theory.

[6] The deeds of an Arahat, a perfect saint, are neither good nor bad because he has gone beyond both good and evil. This does not mean that he is passive. He *is* active, but his activity is selfless and is directed to help others to tread the Path he has trod himself. His deeds, ordinarily accepted as 'good', lack creative power as regards himself, but he is not exempted from the effects of his past actions. He accumulates no fresh kammic activities. Whatever actions he does, as an Arahat, are termed "indeterminate", and are not regarded as Kamma. They are ethically ineffective. Understanding things as they truly are he has finally shattered the cosmic chain of cause and effect.

[7] It should not be misunderstood that Arahats do not sleep. Whether asleep or awake they are regarded as sleepless or vigilant ones, since the five Stimulating Virtues, namely, confidence, energy, mindfulness, concentration, and wisdom, are ever present in them.

[8] The passions.

[9] By conquest is here meant the newly developed insight (*vipassanā*).

[10] For the *jhānas* (absorptions or ecstasies), which the aspirant has

41. Before long, alas! this body will lie upon the ground; cast aside, devoid of consciousness, even as a useless log.[11]

42. Whatever (harm) a foe may do to a foe, or a hater to a hater, an ill-directed mind[12] can do one far greater (harm).

43. What neither mother, nor father, nor any other relative can do, a well-directed mind[13] does and thereby elevates one.

developed. The *jhānas* are highly developed mental states obtained by intensified concentration.

[11] *Kalingaraṃ*, a rotten log which cannot be used for any purpose.

[12] The mind that is directed towards the ten kinds of evil, viz.: 1. killing, 2. stealing, 3. unchastity, 4. lying, 5. slandering, 6. harsh speech, 7. vain talk, 8. covetousness, 9. ill-will, 10. false belief.

[13] The mind that is directed towards the ten kinds of meritorious deeds (*kusala*), viz.: 1. generosity, 2. morality, 3. meditation, 4. reverence, 5. service, 6. transference of merit, 7. rejoicing in others' merit, 8. hearing the Doctrine, 9. seeing Buddhas, and 10. straightening one's right views.

IV. PUPPHAVAGGA. FLOWERS

44. Who will conquer this earth (self),[1] and this realm of *Yama*,[2] and this world[3] together with the gods? Who will investigate the well-taught Path of Virtue,[4] even as an expert (garland-maker) will pluck flowers?

[1] That is, one who will understand this self as it really is.

[2] The woeful states (*duggati*), viz.: hell, animal kingdom, Peta Realm and the Asura Realm. Hell is not permanent according to Buddhism. It is a state of misery as are the two last planes where beings suffer for their past evil actions.

[3] Namely, the world of human beings and the six celestial planes. These seven are regarded as states of bliss (*sugati*).

[4] *Dhammapada*. For other translations of this term, see the Preface. The commentary states that the Path of Virtue here means the thirty-seven Factors of Enlightenment (*Bodhipakkhiya-dhammā*). They are:

(*a*) The four Foundations of Mindfulness (*Satipaṭṭhana*), namely, 1. contemplation of the body, 2. contemplation of the feelings, 3. contemplation of consciousness, and 4. contemplation of phenomena.

(*b*) The four Supreme Efforts, namely, 1. the effort to put away evil that has not arisen, 2. the effort to put away the already arisen evil, 3. the effort to cultivate unrisen good, and 4. the effort to promote risen good.

(*c*) The four Means of Accomplishment (*iddhipāda*), namely, will, energy, thought, and investigation.

(*d*) The five Faculties (*indriya*), namely, confidence, energy, mindfulness, concentration, and wisdom.

(*e*) The five Forces (*bala*), having the same names as the *indriyas*.

(*f*) The seven Factors of Enlightenment (*bojjhanga*), namely, mindfulness, investigation of the truth, energy, joy, serenity, concentration, and equanimity.

(*g*) The Eightfold Path, namely, right views, right thoughts, right speech, right action, right livelihood, right endeavour, right mindfulness, and right concentration.

45. A disciple in training (*sekha*) [5] will conquer this earth, and this realm of Yama together with the realm of the gods; a disciple in training will investigate the well-taught Path of Virtue, even as an expert (garland-maker) will pluck flowers.

46. Knowing that this body is like foam,[6] and comprehending its mirage-nature,[7] one should destroy the flower-shafts [8] of sensual passions (*Māra*) and pass beyond the sight of the King of death.

47. The man who gathers flowers (of sensual pleasures), whose mind is distracted, death carries off as a great flood a sleeping village.

48. The man who gathers flowers (of sensual pleasures), whose mind is distracted, and who is insatiate in desires, the Destroyer [9] brings under his sway.

49. As a bee without harming the flower, its colour or scent, flies away, collecting only the honey, even so should the sage wander [10] in the village.

50. One should not pry into the faults of others, things left done and undone by others, but one's own deeds done and undone.

[5] The term *sekha*, lit., one who is still undergoing training, is applied to a disciple who has attained the first stage of sainthood (*sotāpatti*) until he attains the final *arahatta* fruit stage. When he totally eradicates all passions and attains the fruit stage of an Arahat, he is called an *asekha*, as he has perfected his training.

It is an *asekha* saint who understands this self and the whole world as they really are. There is no graceful English equivalent for this difficult Pāli term.

[6] Owing to its fleeting nature.

[7] Because there is nothing substantial in this body.

[8] Namely, life's sorrow, born of passions. An Arahat destroys all passions by his wisdom and attains Nibbāna where there is no death.

[9] *Antaka*, lit., 'Ender', means death.

[10] Seeking alms, without inconveniencing any.

51. As a flower that is lovely and beautiful, but is scentless, even so fruitless is the well-spoken word of one who does not practise it.

52. As a flower that is lovely, beautiful, and scent-laden, even so fruitful is the well-spoken word of one who practises it.

53. As from a heap of flowers many a garland is made, even so many good deeds should be done by one born a mortal.

54. The perfume of flowers blows not against the wind, nor does the fragrance of sandal-wood, *tagara* [11] and jasmine ; but the fragrance of the virtuous blows against the wind ; the virtuous man pervades every direction.

55. Sandal-wood, *tagara*, lotus, jasmine, above all these kinds of fragrance, the perfume of virtue is by far the best.

56. Of little account is the fragrance of *tagara* or sandal ; the fragrance of the virtuous that blows even amongst the gods is supreme.

57. *Māra* [12] finds not the path of those who are virtuous, careful in living, and freed by right knowledge.

58, 59. As upon a heap of rubbish thrown on the highway, a sweet-smelling, lovely lotus there may grow, even so amongst the rubbish of beings, a disciple of the Fully Enlightened One outshines the blind worldlings with wisdom.

[11] A kind of shrub from which a fragrant powder is obtained.
[12] The personification of evil.

V. BĀLAVAGGA. FOOLS

60. Long is the night to the wakeful; long is the league to the weary; long is *saṃsāra* [1] to the foolish who know not the Sublime Truth.

61. If, as he fares, he meets no companion who is better or equal, let him firmly pursue his solitary career; there is no fellowship with the foolish.[2]

62. "Sons have I; wealth have I": Thus is the fool worried; verily, he himself is not his own. Whence sons? Whence wealth?

63. A fool who thinks that he is a fool is for that very reason a wise man; the fool who thinks that he is wise is called a fool indeed.

64. Though a fool through all his life associates with a wise man, he no more understands the Dhamma than a spoon the flavour of soup.

65. Though an intelligent person only for a moment associates with a wise man, quickly he understands the Dhamma as the tongue the flavour of soup.

66. Fools of little wit move about with the very self as their own foe, doing evil deeds, the fruit of which is bitter.

67. That deed is not well done when after having done it one

[1] Lit., wandering again and again. It is the ocean of life or existence. *Saṃsāra* is defined as the unbroken flow of the stream of aggregates, elements, and sense-faculties.

Saṃsāra is also explained as the "continued flow of the stream of being from life to life, from existence to existence".

[2] Out of compassion, to work for their betterment, one may associate with them.

repents, and when one weeping and with tearful face reaps the fruit thereof.

68. That deed is well done when after having done it one repents not, and when one with joy and pleasure reaps the fruit thereof.

69. As sweet as honey the fool thinks an evil deed, so long as it ripens not; but, when it ripens, then he comes to grief.

70. Month after month, with a kusa-grass blade, a fool may eat his food; but he is not worth a sixteenth part of them who have comprehended the Truth.[3]

71. Verily, an evil deed committed does not immediately bear fruit, just as milk curdles not at once; smouldering, it follows the fool like fire covered with ashes.

72. To his ruin, indeed, the fool gains knowledge and fame; they destroy his bright lot and cleave his head.[4]

73. The fool will desire undue reputation, precedence among monks, authority in the monasteries, honour among other families.

74. Let both laymen and monks think, "by myself was this done; in every work, great or small, let them refer to me." Such is the ambition of the fool; his desires and pride increase.

75. Surely, the path that leads to worldly gain is one, and the path that leads to Nibbāna is another; thus understanding this

[3] *Saṃkhatadhammānaṃ*, "who have well weighed the Law", Max Müller and Burlinghame. "Who well have taken things into account", Mrs. Rhys Davids. "Who have studied the Dhamma noble", Woodward. The commentarial explanation is: "The Ariyas who have realized the four Noble Truths."

The prolonged, so-called meritorious fast of alien ascetics who have not destroyed passions, is not worth the sixteenth part of a solitary day's fast of an Ariya who has realized the four Noble Truths.

[4] That is, his wisdom.

the bhikkhu, the disciple of the Buddha, should not rejoice in worldly favours, but cultivate detachment.[5]

[5] *Viveka*, separation or detachment, is threefold, namely, bodily separation from the crowd (*kāyaviveka*), mental separation from passions (*cittaviveka*), and complete separation from all conditioned things which is Nibbāna (*upadhiviveka*).

VI. PAṆḌITAVAGGA. THE WISE

76. Should one see a wise man, who, like a revealer of treasures, points out faults and reproves, let one associate with such a wise person ; it will be better, not worse, for him who associates with such a one.

77. Let him advise, instruct, and dissuade one from evil ; truly pleasing is he to the good, displeasing is he to the bad.

78. Associate not with evil friends, associate not with mean men ; associate with good friends, associate with noble men.

79. He who imbibes the Dhamma abides in happiness with mind pacified ; the wise man ever delights in the Dhamma revealed by the Ariyas.[1]

80. Irrigators lead the waters ; fletchers bend the shafts ; carpenters bend the wood ; the wise control themselves.

81. As a solid rock is not shaken by the wind, even so the wise are not ruffled by praise or blame.

82. Just as a lake, deep, clear, and still, even so on hearing the teachings the wise become exceedingly peaceful.[2]

83. The good give up (attachment for) everything[3] ; the saintly prattle not with thoughts of craving : whether affected by happiness or by pain, the wise show neither elation nor depression.

84. Neither for the sake of oneself nor for the sake of another (does a wise person do any wrong) ; he should not desire sons,

[1] *Ariya*, which means 'one who is far removed from passions', was originally a racial term ; in Buddhism it indicates nobility of character, and is invariably applied to the Buddhas and Arahats.

[2] By attaining saintship.

[3] The five Aggregates, etc. See v. 203.

wealth, or kingdom (by doing wrong); by unjust means he should not desire his own success. Then (only) such a one is indeed virtuous, wise, and righteous.

85. Few are there amongst men who go to the Further Shore[4]; the rest of this mankind only run about on the bank.[5]

86. But those who rightly act according to the teaching, which is well expounded, those are they who will reach the Further Shore (crossing) the realm of passions,[6] so hard to cross.

87, 88. Coming from home to the homeless, the wise man should abandon dark states and cultivate the bright.[7] He should seek great delight in detachment (Nibbāna), so hard to enjoy. Giving up sensual pleasures, with no impediments,[8] the wise man should cleanse himself of the impurities of the mind.

89. Whose minds are well perfected in the factors of Enlightenment,[9]—who, without clinging, delight in 'the giving up of grasping'[10] (i.e. Nibbāna), they, the corruption-free,[11] shining ones, have attained Nibbāna even in this world.[12]

[4] Namely, Nibbāna.

[5] Namely, self-illusion (*sakkāyadiṭṭhi*). The majority are born again in this world.

[6] *Maccudheyya*, i.e. worldly existence where passions dominate.

[7] The dark states are the ten kinds of evil deeds, and the bright states are the ten kinds of good deeds. See note on v. 43.

[8] The five Hindrances (*nīvaraṇa*) that obstruct the way to deliverance. They are sense-desires (*kāmacchanda*), ill-will (*vyāpāda*), sloth and torpor (*thīnamiddha*), restlessness and brooding (*uddhacca-kukkucca*), and indecision (*vicikiccha*). See *A Manual of Buddhism* by the writer.

[9] See v. 44.

[10] There are four kinds of 'grasping', namely, sense-desires, false beliefs, adherence to wrongful rites and ceremonies, self-illusion.

[11] There are four kinds of Corruptions (*āsavas*), viz. sensual pleasures (*kāma*), becoming (*bhava*), false views (*diṭṭhi*) and ignorance (*avijjā*). The first *āsava* is attachment to the sentient realm, the second is attachment to the Realm of Form and the Formless Realms.

[12] On attaining Arahatship, the final stage of Sainthood, one eradicates

all impurities and realizes Nibbāna in this very life. This is known as the *sopādisesa Nibbāna*—i.e. experiencing Nibbānic bliss with the body remaining. The Arahat lives as long as the power of his rebirth reproductive *kamma* lasts, just as the spinning wheel rotates even when the hand is removed. After death he attains *anupādisesa Nibbāna*—i.e. Nibbāna without the body. See *A Manual of Buddhism* and *The Buddha-Dhamma* by the writer.

VII. ARAHANTAVAGGA. THE ARAHAT[1]

90. For him who has completed the journey, for him who is sorrowless,[2] for him who from everything is wholly free,[3] for him who has destroyed all Ties,[4] the fever (of passion) exists not.[5]

91. The mindful exert themselves; to no abode are they attached; like swans that quit their pools, home after home they abandon (and go).[6]

92. They for whom there is no accumulation,[7] who reflect well over their food, whose object is the Void, the Signless,[8] Deliverance—their course cannot be traced, like that of birds in air.

[1] An Arahat, lit., 'worthy one', is a perfect saint, who has destroyed all passions such as lust, hatred, and ignorance. After death he is born no more, but attains *parinibbāna.*

[2] One gives up sorrow on attaining the third stage of Sainthood, that of the *anāgāmi,* one who is not born again in this world.

[3] That is, with no attachment to anything.

[4] There are four kinds of *ganthas* or ties, viz.: 1. covetousness (*abhijjhā*), 2. ill-will (*vyāpāda*), 3. indulgence in wrongful rites and ceremonies (*sīlabbataparāmāsa*), and 4. adherence to one's dogma (*idaṃ saccabhinivesa*).

[5] This verse refers to the ethical state of an arahat.

Heat is both physical and mental. An arahat experiences bodily heat as long as he is alive, but is not thereby worried. Mental heat of passions he experiences not.

[6] Arahats wander whithersoever they like without any attachment to any particular place, as they are free from the conception of 'I and mine'.

[7] Kammic activities and requisites.

[8] Nibbāna is Deliverance (*vimokkha*). It is called Void because it is void of lust, hatred, and ignorance. It is signless because it is free from the signs of lust, etc. Arahats experience nibbanic bliss whilst alive.

93. He whose corruptions are destroyed, he who is not attached to food, he whose object is the Void, the Signless, Deliverance, his path cannot be traced, like that of birds in air.

94. He whose senses are subdued, like steeds well trained by a charioteer; he whose pride is destroyed and is free from the corruptions, such steadfast ones even the gods hold dear.

95. Like the earth, like an *indakhīla*,[9] a balanced and well-conducted person is not resentful; like a pool unsullied by mud is he; to such a stable one[10] life's wanderings are no more.[11]

96. Calm is the mind, calm is the speech, and action and right knowledge of him who is wholly freed,[12] perfectly peaceful,[13] and who is such a stable one.

97. The man who is not credulous,[14] who understands the uncreate[15] (Nibbāna), who has cut off the links,[16] who has put

[9] By *indakhīla* is meant either a column as firm and high as that of Sakka's, or the chief column that stands at the entrance to a city.

Commentators mention that these *indakhīlas* are firm posts which are erected either inside or outside the city as an embellishment. Usually they are made of bricks or durable wood in octangular shapes. Half of the post is embedded in the earth, hence the metaphor as firm and steady as an *indakhīla*.

[10] *Tādi* is one who has neither attachment to desirable objects nor aversion to undesirable objects. Nor does he cling to anything. Amidst the eight worldly conditions, gain and loss, fame and defame, blame and praise, happiness and pain, an arahat remains unperturbed, manifesting neither attachment nor aversion, neither elation nor depression.

[11] As they are not subject to birth and death.

[12] From all defilements.

[13] Since his mind is absolutely pure.

[14] *Assaddho*, lit., unfaithful. He does not merely accept from other sources because he himself knows by personal experience.

[15] *Akata*, Nibbāna is called *akata* because it is not created by anyone.

[16] The links of existence and rebirth.

an end [17] to occasion (of good and evil), who has vomited all desires, he, indeed, is a supreme man.[18]

98. Whether in village or in forest, in vale or on hill,[19] wherever arahats dwell, delightful, indeed, is that spot.

99. Delightful are the forests where worldlings delight not; the passionless will rejoice therein, they seek no sensual pleasures.[20]

[17] By means of the four Paths of Sainthood. Gross forms of desires are eradicated at the first three stages, the subtle forms at the last stage.

[18] This is an example of an Indian riddle, and is discussed in the Introduction, p. 8.

[19] *Ninna* and *thala*, lit., low-lying and elevated grounds.

[20] The passionless arahats rejoice in secluded forests which have no attraction for worldlings.

VIII. SAHASSAVAGGA. THOUSANDS

100. Better than a thousand utterances with useless words is one single beneficial word, by hearing which one is pacified.

101. Better than a thousand verses with useless words is one beneficial single line, by hearing which one is pacified.

102. Should one recite a hundred verses with useless words, better is one single word of the Dhamma, by hearing which one is pacified.

103. Though he should conquer a thousand thousand [1] men in the battlefield, yet he, indeed, is the noblest victor who should conquer himself.

104, 105. Self-conquest is, indeed, far greater than the conquest of all other folk; neither a god nor a *gandhabba*,[2] nor *Māra* [3] with *Brahmā*,[4] can win back the victory of such a person who is self-subdued and ever lives in restraint.

106. Though month after month with a thousand, one should make an offering for a hundred years, yet, if only for a moment, one should honour one whose self has been well trained, that honour is, indeed, better than a century of sacrifice.

107. Though a man for a century should tend the (sacred) fire in the forest, yet, if only for a moment, he should honour one whose self has been well trained, that honour is, indeed, better than a century of sacrifice.

[1] *Sahassaṃ sahassena*, a thousand reckoned by a thousand, that is, ten lakhs. (Cy.)

[2] A class of beings who are supposed to be heavenly musicians.

[3] Here *Māra* is used in the sense of a god.

[4] Another class of beings, even superior to the gods in the heaven of Sakka who have developed *jhānas* (ecstasies).

108. In this world whatever gift or alms [5] a person seeking merit should offer for a year, all that is not worth a single quarter. Better is homage towards the Upright.[6]

109. For one who frequently honours and respects elders,[7] four things increase: age, beauty, bliss,[8] and strength.[9]

110. Though he should live a hundred years, immoral and uncontrolled, yet better, indeed, is it to live one single day, virtuous and meditative.

111. Though one should live a hundred years, without wisdom and control, yet better, indeed, is the single day's life of one who is moral and meditative.

112. Though one should live a hundred years, idle and inactive, yet better, indeed, is the single day's life of one who makes an intense effort.

113. Though one should live a hundred years, without comprehending rising and passing away,[10] yet better, indeed, is the single day's life of one who comprehends rising and passing away.

114. Though one should live a hundred years, without seeing the deathless state,[11] yet better, indeed, is the single day's life of one who sees the deathless state.

[5] According to the commentary *iṭṭhaṃ* is that which is given on festival occasions, and *hutaṃ* is that which is prepared and given either to guests or with a belief in kamma and its results.

The idea conveyed by this stanza is that reverence paid to a saint is far superior to gifts and alms given to worldlings.

[6] The saints, such as *sotāpannas* (stream-winners), etc.

[7] Those who are advanced in age and virtue.

[8] Physical and mental happiness.

[9] Physical and mental vigour.

[10] The rise and decay of mind and matter, namely, the impermanence of all conditioned things. A disciple of the Buddha is expected to contemplate the fleeting nature of life, so that he may not be attached to illusory material pleasures.

[11] *Amataṃ padaṃ*, the unconditioned state of Nibbāna, free from birth, decay, and death.

115. Though one should live a hundred years, not seeing the Truth sublime [12]; yet better, indeed, is the single day's life of one who sees the Truth sublime.

[12] The nine Supramundane States, namely, the four Paths, the four Fruits of Sanctification, and Nibbāna.

IX. PĀPAVAGGA. EVIL

116. Make haste in doing good [1]; check your mind from evil [2]; for the mind of him who is slow in doing merit delights in evil.

117. Should a person commit evil, he should not do it again and again; he should not find pleasure therein; painful is the accumulation of evil.

118. Should a person perform merit,[3] he should do it again and again; he should find pleasure therein: blissful is the accumulation of merit.

119. Even an evil-doer sees good so long as evil ripens not; but when it bears fruit, then he sees the evil results.[4]

120. Even a good person sees evil so long as good ripens not; but when it bears fruit, then the good one sees the good results.[5]

[1] There should be no delay in doing good deeds. One must avail oneself of every opportunity to do good. Every effort should be made to control the mind as it is prone to evil. The impure mind rejoices in evil thoughts.

[2] *Pāpa*, evil, is that which defiles one's mind. It is that which leads to woeful states. What is associated with attachment, ill-will, and delusion is evil. There are ten kinds of evil.

[3] *Puññā*, merit, is that which cleanses one's mind. *Kusala* is another term for *puññā*. There are ten kinds of meritorious deeds. See note on vv. 42, 43.

[4] A wicked person may lead a prosperous life as the result of his past good deeds. He will experience happiness owing to the potentiality of his past good over the present evil, a seeming injustice which often prevails in this world. When once, according to the inexorable law of kamma, his evil actions fructify, then he perceives the painful effects of his wickedness.

[5] A virtuous person, as it often happens, may meet with adversity,

121. Despise not evil, saying, "It will not come nigh unto me"; by the falling of drops even a water-jar is filled; likewise the fool, gathering little by little, fills himself with evil.

122. Despise not merit, saying, "It will not come nigh unto me"; even by the falling of drops a water-jar is filled; likewise the wise man, gathering little by little, fills himself with good.

123. Just as a merchant, with a small escort and great wealth, avoids a perilous way, just as one desiring to live avoids poison, even so should one shun evil things.

124. If no wound there be in the hand, one may carry poison in it; poision does not affect one who has no wound; there is no ill for him who does no wrong.

125. Whoever offends a harmless person, one pure and guiltless, upon that very fool the evil recoils like fine dust thrown against the wind.

126. Some are born in a womb [6]; evil-doers in hell [7]; the pious go to Heaven [8]; Undefiled Ones pass away into Nibbāna.[9]

127. Not in the sky, nor in mid-ocean, nor on entering a

owing to the potentiality of his past evil actions over his present good acts. He is convinced of the efficacy of his present good deeds only when, at the opportune moment, they fructify giving him abundant bliss.

The fact that at times the wicked are prosperous and the virtuous are unfortunate is itself a strong evidence to believe in kamma and rebirth.

[6] According to Buddhism there are four kinds of birth, namely, egg-born (*andaja*), womb-born (*jalābuja*), moisture-born (*saṃsedaja*), and spontaneous birth (*opapātika*).

[7] *Niraya* = *ni* + *aya* = devoid of happiness. It is not an eternal state. There are four kinds of *niraya*, viz. hell (*apāya*), animal kingdom (*tiracchānayoni*), plane of petas (*petayoni*), and the plane of asuras demons (*asurayoni*). They are not eternal but temporary woeful states.

[8] *Sagga* = *su* + *agga* = full of happiness.

[9] Arahats, after death, are not born any more, but attain Parinibbāna.

mountain cave, is found that place on earth, where abiding one may escape from (the consequences of) an evil deed.[10]

128. Not in the sky, nor in mid-ocean, nor on entering a mountain cave, is found that place on earth where abiding one will not be overcome by death.

[10] The Buddhist law of causation cannot be bribed, nor can one escape the evil consequences of kamma by seeking refuge in any place on earth. No god or even a Buddha can intervene in the operation of kamma.

X. DAṆḌAVAGGA. PUNISHMENT, OR THE ROD

129. All tremble at punishment. All fear death ; comparing others with oneself, one should neither kill nor cause to kill.

130. All tremble at punishment. Life is dear to all ; comparing others with oneself, one should neither kill nor cause to kill.

131. Whoever seeking his own happiness, harms with rod pleasure-loving beings gets no happiness hereafter.

132. Whoever seeking his own happiness, harms not with rod pleasure-loving beings gets happiness hereafter.

133. Speak not harshly to anyone ; those thus addressed will retort ; painful, indeed, is vindictive speech ; blows in exchange may bruise you.

134. If, like a broken gong, you silence yourself, you have already attained Nibbāna ; no vindictiveness will be found in you.

135. As with a staff the herdsman drives kine to pasture, even so do old age and death drive out the lives of beings.

136. So when a fool does wrong deeds, he does not realize (their evil nature) ; by his own deeds the stupid man is tormented, like one burnt by fire.

137. He who with rod harms the rodless and harmless,[1] soon will come to one of these states :

138–140. He will be subject to acute pain,[2] disaster, bodily injury, or even grievous sickness, or loss of mind, or oppression by the king, or heavy accusation, or loss of relatives, or destruction of wealth,[3] or ravaging fire that will burn his houses. Upon the dissolution of the body this unwise man will be born in hell.

[1] Namely, Arahats who are weaponless and innocent.

[2] That might cause death.

[3] Loss in business transactions, loss in wealth, etc.

141. Not wandering naked,[4] nor matted locks,[5] nor filth,[6] nor fasting,[7] nor lying on the ground,[8] nor dust,[9] nor ashes,[10] nor squatting on the heels,[11] purify a mortal who has not overcome doubts.[12]

142. Though gaily decked, if he should live in peace, (with passions) subdued (and senses) controlled, certain [13] (of the four Paths of Saintship), perfectly pure,[14] laying aside the rod towards all living beings,[15] a Brahman [16] indeed is he, an ascetic [17] is he, a bhikkhu [18] is he.[19]

[4] Naked asceticism is still practised in India. External dirtiness is regarded by some as a mark of saintliness. The Buddha denounces such external forms of strict asceticism. The members of his celibate Order follow a middle path, avoiding the extremes of self-mortification and self-indulgence. Simplicity, humility, and poverty should be the marked characteristics of bhikkhus as much as cleanliness.

[5] Unwashed matted hair is regarded as a mark of holiness.

[6] The non-cleansing of teeth, smearing the body with mud, etc.

[7] Fasting alone does not tend to purification. The bhikkhus too fast daily after midday till the following dawn.

[8] Sleeping on the ground. Bhikkhus only avoid luxurious and high couches.

[9] Through not bathing.

[10] Rubbing the body with ashes is still practised by some ascetics.

[11] Continually sitting and wandering in that posture.

[12] With regard to the Buddha, Dhamma, Sangha, etc.

[13] *Niyata*, the four paths are *sotāpatti*, *sakadāgāmi*, *anāgāmi*, and *arahatta*.

[14] Mrs. Rhys Davids, " Walking in God ", a very misleading phrase, totally foreign to Buddhism. The commentarial explanation is *seṭṭhacariya*—highest conduct.

[15] Absolutely harmless towards all.

[16] Because he has cast aside impurities.

[17] *Samaṇa*, because he has controlled impurities.

[18] *Bhikkhu*, because he has destroyed passions.

[19] A gaily decked minister, stricken with grief, listened to the Buddha, seated on an elephant. On hearing the discourse he realized arahatship. Simultaneous with his realization his death occurred. The Buddha then

143. (Rarely) is found in this world anyone who, restrained by modesty, avoids reproach, as a thorough-bred horse the whip.[20]

144. Like a thorough-bred horse, touched by the whip, even so be strenuous and zealous. By confidence, by virtue, by effort, by concentration, by the investigation of the Truth, by being endowed with knowledge and conduct,[21] and by being mindful, get rid of this great suffering.

145. Irrigators lead the waters; fletchers bend the shafts; carpenters bend the wood; the virtuous control themselves.[22]

advised his followers to pay him the respect due to an arahat. When the bhikkhus questioned him how the minister could have attained arahatship in such elegant dress the Buddha uttered this verse to show that purity comes from within and not from without. In striking contrast to the former this verse clearly indicates the Buddhist view of a holy person. It is not the apparel that counts but internal purity.

[20] A self-respecting bhikkhu or layman, when obsessed with evil thoughts, tries to eradicate them there and then. This verse indicates that such persons are rare.

[21] *Vijjācaraṇa*—eight kinds of knowledge and fifteen kinds of conduct.

[22] Cf. v. 80.

XI. JARĀVAGGA. OLD AGE

146. What is laughter, what is joy, when the world is ever burning? Shrouded by darkness, do you not seek a light?[1]

147. Behold this beautiful body, a mass of sores, a heaped-up (lump), diseased, much thought of,[2] in which nothing lasts, nothing persists.

148. Thoroughly worn out is this body, a nest of diseases, perishable; this putrid mass breaks up, truly, life ends in death.

149. Like gourds cast away in autumn are these dove-hued bones. What pleasure is there in looking at them?

150. Of bones is (this) city made, plastered with flesh and blood. Herein are stored decay, death, conceit, and detraction.[3]

151. Even ornamented royal chariots wear out; so too the body reaches old age; but the Dhamma[4] of the Good grows not old; thus do the Good[5] reveal (it) among the Good.

152. The man of little learning grows old like the bull: his muscles grow, his wisdom grows not.

[1] Visākhā, the chief lay benefactress of the Buddha, once visited him, accompanied by some women who, without her knowledge, had become drunk. In their drunken state they discourteously danced and sang before the Buddha. By his psychic powers the Buddha created a darkness which brought them to their senses. The Buddha then uttered this verse.

This world is perpetually consumed with the flames of the passions. It is completely shrouded by the veil of ignorance. Being placed in such a world, the wise should try to seek the light of wisdom.

[2] As good and pleasant.

[3] *Makkha*, concealing others' virtues.

[4] The nine Supramundane States: the four Paths, the four Fruits, and Nibbāna.

[5] Such as the Buddhas.

153, 154. Through many a birth I wandered in saṃsāra,[6]
Seeking, but not finding, the builder of the house.
Sorrowful is birth again and again.
O House-builder! Thou art seen. Thou shalt build no house again. All thy rafters are broken, thy ridge-pole is shattered.
My mind has attained the unconditioned, achieved is the end of cravings.

155. They who have not led the Holy Life, who in youth have not acquired wealth, pine away like old herons on a pond without fish.

156. They who have not led the Holy Life, who in youth have not acquired wealth, lie like worn-out bows, sighing after the past.

[6] These two verses, the first paean of Joy (*Udāna*) uttered by the Buddha, immediately after his Enlightenment, are not found elsewhere. As the venerable Ānanda heard them from the mouth of the Buddha they have been inserted here.

Here the Buddha admits his past wanderings in existence which entails suffering, a fact which evidently proves the belief in rebirth. He was compelled to wander, and consequently to suffer as long as he could not discover the architect that built this house, the body. In his final birth he discovered by his own intuitive wisdom the elusive architect residing not outside but within the recesses of his own heart. It was craving or attachment (*taṇhā*), a self-creation, a mental element latent in all. The discovery of the architect is the eradication of craving by attaining Arahatship which in this utterance is alluded to as the end of craving.

The rafters of this self-created house are the defilements (*kilesa*). The ridge-pole that supports the rafters is ignorance (*avijjā*), the root cause of all defilements. The shattering of the ridge-pole of ignorance by wisdom results in the complete demolition of the house. The ridge-pole and rafters are the material with which the architect builds this undesired house. With their destruction the architect is deprived of the wherewithal to rebuild the house which is not wanted. With the demolition of the house the mind attains the unconditioned which is Nibbāna.

XII. ATTAVAGGA. THE SELF[1]

157. If one hold one's self dear,[2] one should protect oneself well; during any of the three watches the wise man should keep vigil.

158. Let one first establish one's self in what is proper, and then instruct others. Such a wise man will not get defiled.

159. As he instructs others so should he himself act; himself fully controlled, he should control (others); for the self indeed is difficult to control.

160. The self is lord of the self: for what other lord would there be? For with self well controlled one obtains a lord difficult to gain.

161. By one's self alone is evil done; it is self-born, it is self-caused; evil grinds the unwise as a diamond a hard gem.

162. He who is exceedingly corrupt, like a māluvā creeper strangling a sal tree, does to himself what even an enemy would wish for him.

163. Easy to do are things that are bad and not beneficial to oneself, but very, very difficult indeed to do is that which is beneficial and good.

164. The stupid man, who on account of false views scorns the teaching of the arahats, the noble ones, and the Righteous, ripens like the fruits of the kashta reed, only for his own destruction.

[1] According to Buddhism there is no permanent soul or unchanging entity (*atta*) either created by a god or emanating from a *Paramātman*. Here the term *atta* (self) is applied by the Buddha to the whole body, or one's personality or mind or life flux.

[2] That is, if one values oneself.

165. By oneself, indeed, is evil done; by oneself is one defiled [3]; by oneself is evil left undone; by oneself, indeed, is one purified. Purity and impurity depend on oneself. No one purifies another.

166. Because of others' well-being, howsoever great, let not one neglect his own welfare [4]; clearly perceiving his own welfare, let him be intent on his own goal.

[3] Or defiles.

[4] Personal sanctification.

As the Buddha was about to pass away his disciples flocked from far and near to pay their respects to him. One Thera named Attadattha, instead of joining them, retired to his cell and meditated. The other bhikkhus reported this matter to the Buddha. When questioned as to his conduct the Thera replied, "Lord, as you would be passing away three months hence I thought the best way to honour you is by attaining Arahatship during your lifetime itself." The Buddha then praised him for his exemplary conduct and recited this verse.

Personal sanctification should not be sacrificed for the sake of external homage.

One must not misunderstand this verse to mean that one should not selflessly work for the weal of others. Selfless service is highly commended by the Buddha.

XIII. LOKAVAGGA. THE WORLD

167. Do not serve mean ends [1]; do not live in heedlessness; do not embrace false views; do not be a world-upholder.[2]

168. Be not heedless in standing (at doors for alms); observe scrupulously (this) practice; he who observes this practice lives happily both in this world and the next.

169. Observe scrupulously (this) practice; do not observe it unscrupulously; he who observes this practice lives happily both in this world and the next.[3]

170. Just as one would view a bubble, just as one would view a mirage; if a person thus looks upon the world,[4] the King of Death sees him not.

171. Come, behold this world, like an ornamented royal chariot, wherein fools flounder, but for the wise there is no attachment.

[1] i.e. sensual pleasures.

[2] By being subject to repeated births and deaths.

[3] On the day after his arrival in his birthplace, immediately after his Enlightenment, he went in quest of alms in the city. King Suddhodana, his father, hearing that his son was seeking alms in the city, excitedly ran up to him and said that he was disgracing him by begging alms in the streets where he formerly used to travel in golden palanquins. Thereupon the Buddha remarked that it was the custom of all his predecessors to go seeking alms from door to door, and he uttered these two verses.

The above translation of vv. 168, 169 is according to the commentary, but owing to the ambiguity of the first word it may be translated, " be alert, be not heedless ", etc.

[4] This psychophysical organism as empty as a bubble and as illusive as a mirage. Such a right-seeing person would end the ills of life.

172. Whoever was heedless before and afterwards is not, such a one illumines this world like the moon freed from clouds.

173. Whoever, by good deed, covers the evil done, such a one illumines the world like the moon freed from clouds.

174. Blind is this world; few are there who clearly see; as birds that escape from a net few go to heaven.[5]

175. Swans go on the path of the sun; (men) go through air by psychic powers.[6] The wise are led away from the world,[7] having conquered Māra and his host.[8]

176. There is no evil that cannot be done by a lying person, who has transgressed the one law (of truthfulness) and who is indifferent to a world beyond.[9]

177. Verily, the misers go not to celestial realms. Fools do not indeed praise liberality; the wise man rejoices in giving and thereby becomes happy thereafter.

178. Better than sole sovereignty over the earth,[10] better than

[5] *Sagga*, blissful states, not places of eternal happiness.

[6] *Iddhi*. By mental development it is possible to fly through the air, walk on water, dive into the earth, etc. Such kinds of powers are psychic and supernormal, but not miraculous.

[7] That is, the Arahats attain Nibbāna.

[8] The host of Māra, the Evil One, is described as ten kinds of passions. They are: 1. Material pleasures (*kāma*), 2. aversion for the Holy Life, (*arati*), 3, hunger and thirst (*khuppipāsa*), 4. craving (*taṇhā*), 5. sloth and torpor (*thīna-middha*), 6. fear (*bhaya*), 7. doubt (*vicikicchā*), 8. distraction and obstinacy (*makkha, thambha*), 9. gain (*lābha*), praise (*siloka*), honour (*sakkāra*), and fame (*yasa*), 10. extolling of oneself and the contempt of others (*attukkaṃsana paravambhanā*).

[9] An untruthful person, with no self-respect, who has no belief in an after-life and who has no fear for the attendant consequences of evil, is liable to commit any evil. Such a person does not see earthly bliss or heavenly bliss or Nibbanic bliss. (Cy.)

[10] Internal purification is far superior to fleeting worldly possessions or transitory heavenly bliss.

going to heaven, better than even lordship over all the worlds is the Fruit of a Stream-winner.[11]

[11] *Sotāpatti*, attainment to the stream that leads to Nibbāna, i.e. the first stage of Sainthood. The Stream-winners are not born in woeful states, but the worldly great are not exempt from them.

XIV. BUDDHAVAGGA. THE BUDDHA

179. Him whose conquest (of passion) is not turned into defeat,[1] whose conquest no one in the world approaches,[2] him, the trackless Buddha of infinite range—by what way will you lead him? [3]

180. Him in whom there is not that entangling, embroiling craving to lead (to any life), him the trackless Buddha of infinite range—by what way will you lead him? [4]

181. Those wise ones who are absorbed in meditation, who delight in the stillness of renunciation (i.e. Nibbāna), such mindful perfect Buddhas even the gods hold (most) dear.

182. Hard is the attaining of birth as a man, hard the life of mortals, hard the hearing of the Sublime Truth, hard the appearance of Buddhas.

183. Not to do any evil, to cultivate good,[5] to purify one's mind, this is the teaching of the Buddhas.[6]

184. Forbearing patience is the highest devotion,[7] Nibbāna is supreme say the Buddhas; he, verily, is not a recluse [8] who harms another; nor is he an ascetic [9] who troubles others.

[1] Being devoid of lust, etc.

[2] Because the eradicated passions do not rise again.

[3] *Nessatha*, will you lead to temptation.

[4] Both these verses were uttered by the Buddha when the three daughters of Māra the Evil One made a vain attempt to entice him by their female charms.

[5] What is associated with the roots of attachment, ill-will, and delusion is evil; what is associated with their opposites, generosity, goodwill, and wisdom, is good.

[6] The Word of the Buddha is summarized in this verse. [7] *Tapo.*

[8] *Pabbajito*, one who casts aside one's impurities, and has left the world.

[9] *Samaṇo*—one who subdues one's passions; an ascetic.

185. Not insulting, not harming, restraint according to the Fundamental Moral Code,[10] moderation in food, secluded above, intent on the higher consciousness,[11] this is the teaching of the Buddhas.

186, 187. Not by a shower of gold coins does contentment arise in sensual pleasures. Of little sweetness, but painful, are sensual pleasures. Knowing thus, the wise man finds no delight even in heavenly pleasures. The disciple of the Fully Enlightened One delights in the destruction of craving.

188. To many a refuge fear-stricken men betake themselves, to hills, woods, gardens, trees, and shrines.

189. Nay, no such refuge is safe, no such refuge is supreme ; not by resorting to such a refuge is one freed from all ill.

190–192. He who has gone for refuge [12] to the Buddha, the Dhamma, and the Sangha, sees with right knowledge the four Noble Truths, Sorrow, the Cause of Sorrow, the Transcending of Sorrow, and the Noble Eightfold Path which leads to the Cessation of Sorrow.

[10] *Pātimokkha*—these are the 220 chief rules (excluding the seven ways of settling disputes) which every bhikkhu is expected to observe.

[11] *Adhicitta.* The eight Attainments (*aṭṭhasamāpatti*), the four *rūpa jhānas* and the four *arūpa jhānas.* They are higher stages of mental concentration, which enable one to gain supernormal powers.

[12] One's best refuge is oneself. A Buddhist seeks refuge in the Buddha, the Dhamma, and the Sangha as the Teacher, the Teaching and the Taught in order to gain his deliverance. The Buddha is the supreme instructor who shows the way to deliverance. The Dhamma is the unique way. The Sangha represents the taught who have followed the way and have become living examples. One formally becomes a Buddhist by intelligently seeking refuge in this Triple Gem (*Tisaraṇa*).

A Buddhist does not seek refuge in the Buddha with the hope that he will be saved by his personal deliverance. The confidence of a follower of the Buddha is like that of a sick person in a noted physician, or a student in his teacher.

This indeed is refuge secure ; this indeed is refuge supreme. By reaching such refuge one is released from all sorrow.

193. Hard to find is a "thorough-bred" man [13] : he is not born everywhere ; where such a man is born that family thrives happily.

194. Happy is the birth of Buddhas ; happy is the teaching of the Sublime Dhamma ; happy is the unity of the Sangha [14] ; happy is the devotion of the united ones.

195, 196. He who reverences those worthy of reverence, whether the Buddhas or disciples ; those who have overcome passions and have got rid of grief and lamentation ; the merit of him who reverences such peaceful and fearless Ones cannot be measured by anyone as such and such.

[13] *Purisājañña,* a Buddha.

[14] *Sangha* is the oldest historic celibate Order, founded by the Buddha. It is "democratic in constitution and communistic in distribution". Strictly speaking, the Sangha is constituted by those noble disciples who have realized the four Paths and the four Fruits. The ordinary bhikkhus of the present day are merely their representatives.

XV. SUKHAVAGGA. HAPPINESS

197. Ah, happily do we live without hate amongst the hateful; amidst hateful men we dwell unhating.

198. Ah, happily do we live in good health amongst the ailing; amidst ailing men we dwell in good health.[1]

199. Ah, happily do we live without yearning (for sensual pleasures) amongst those who yearn (for them); amidst those who yearn (for them) we dwell without yearning.

200. Ah, happily do we live, we who have no impediments [2]; feeders of joy shall we be even as the gods of the Radiant Realm.[3]

201. Victory breeds hatred; the defeated live in pain. Happily the peaceful live, giving up victory and defeat.

202. There is no fire like lust, no crime [4] like hate; there is no ill like the body,[5] no bliss higher than Peace (Nibbāna).

203. Hunger [6] is the greatest disease, compound things [7] the

[1] Free from the disease of passions.

[2] *Kiñcana*, such as lust, hatred, etc., which act as hindrances.

[3] Once the Buddha, due to a plot of Māra the Evil One, was compelled to starve, as he did not obtain anything when he went in quest of alms. Seeing the Buddha with an empty bowl Māra jokingly remarked that the Buddha was evidently afflicted with hunger.

Thereupon the Buddha recited this verse.

[4] *Kali* = sin.

[5] *Pañcakkhandha*, the five Aggregates.

[6] Ordinary diseases are usually curable by one remedy, but hunger has to be appeased daily.

[7] Here *Sankhārā* is used in the sense of *khandhā*, the five Aggregates—namely, the body (*rūpa*), feelings (*vedanā*), perception (*saññā*), mental states (*sankhārā*), and consciousness (*viññāna*). The so-called being consists of these five constituent parts. Both *khandha* and *sankhārā* are used to denote these five conditioned things.

greatest ill; knowing this as it really is (the wise realize) Nibbāna, the bliss supreme.

204. Health is the highest gain; contentment is the greatest wealth; kinsmen [8] are the best in whom to trust; Nibbāna is the chiefest bliss.

205. Having tasted the flavour of seclusion and the flavour of Nibbāna's Peace, woeless and stainless becomes he, drinking the taste of the joy of the Dhamma.

206. Good is the sight of Ariyas: their company is ever happy; by not seeing fools one may ever be happy.

207. Truly he who moves in company with fools grieves for a long time; association with fools is ever painful as with a foe. Happy is association with the wise, even like meeting with kinsfolk.

208. With the intelligent, the wise, the learned, the devout, the dutiful and the Ariya—with such a virtuous, intellectual man should one associate, as the moon follows its course among the stars.

[8] Whether related or not.

XVI. PIYAVAGGA. AFFECTIONS

209. Attaching oneself to that which should be avoided,[1] not attaching oneself to that which should be pursued,[2] giving up the quest,[3] one who goes after pleasure envies him who exerts himself.[4]

210. Consort not with those that are dear,[5] nor ever with those that are not dear ; not seeing those that are dear and the sight of those that are not dear, are both painful.[6]

211. Hence hold nothing dear, for separation from those that are dear is bad : bonds do not exist for those to whom nought is dear or not dear.

212. From endearment springs grief, from endearment springs fear ; for him who is wholly free from endearment there is no grief, much less fear.

213. From affection springs grief, from affection springs fear ; for him who is wholly free from affection there is no grief, much less fear.

214. From delight springs grief, from delight springs fear ; for him who is wholly free from delight there is no grief, much less fear.

215. From lust springs grief, from lust springs fear ; for him

[1] That is, frequenting places undesirable for bhikkhus.

[2] That is, to right attention (*yoniso manasikāra*). (Cy.)

[3] The practice of higher Morality, Concentration, and Meditation.

[4] The bhikkhu, with no right discrimination, gives up his quest, and being attached to sensual pleasures, returns to lay life. Later he sees successful bhikkhus and envies them.

[5] Applicable to both animate and inanimate objects, pleasant persons or things.

[6] Attachment in one case and aversion in the other.

who is wholly free from lust there is no grief, much less fear.

216. From craving springs grief, from craving springs fear; for him who is wholly free from craving there is no grief, much less fear.

217. Whoso is perfect in virtue and insight, is established in the Dhamma,[7] has realized the Truths,[8] and fulfils his own duties,[9] him do folk hold dear.

218. He who has developed a wish for the Undeclared[10] (*Nibbāna*), he whose mind is thrilled (with the three Fruits),[11] he whose mind is not bound by material pleasures, such a person is called an "Upstream-bound One".[12]

219. A man long absent and returned safe from afar, kinsmen, friends, and well-wishers welcome on his arrival.

220. Likewise, his good deeds too will receive the doer who has gone from this world to the next, as kinsmen will receive a dear one on his return.

[7] Nine Supramundane States. See p. 39.

[8] *Saccavādinaṃ*, "speaketh truth", Mrs. Rhys Davids. The four Noble Truths are implied here.

[9] The three modes of discipline, Morality (*sīla*), Concentration (*samādhi*), and Wisdom (*paññā*).

[10] *Anakkhāta* = Nibbāna. It is so called because it should not be said that Nibbāna was created by any or of some such form as blue, etc. (Cy.)

[11] The first three stages of Sainthood.

[12] *Uddhaṃsota*. The reference is to the *Anāgāmis* (Non-Returners) who, after death, are born in the Pure Abodes (*Suddhāvāsa*).

XVII. KODHAVAGGA. ANGER

221. One should give up anger ; one should abandon pride ; one should overcome all fetters.[1] Ills never befall him who clings not to mind and body and is passionless.

222. Whoso, as a rolling chariot, checks his uprisen anger, him I call a charioteer ; other folk merely hold the reins.

223. Conquer anger by love ; conquer evil by good ; conquer the stingy one by giving ; conquer the liar by truth.

224. One should utter the truth ; one should not be angry ; one should give even from a scanty store to him who asks [2] ; by these three things one may go to the presence of the gods.

225. Those sages who are harmless, and are ever restrained in body, go to the deathless state,[3] where gone they never grieve.

226. The Defilements [4] of those who are ever vigilant, who train themselves day and night, who are wholly intent on Nibbāna, fade away.

227. This, O Atula,[5] is an old saying, it is not only of today : they blame those who sit silent, they blame those who speak too much ; those speaking little too they blame ; in this world no one is there unblamed.

228. There never was, there never will be, nor does there exist now, a person who is wholly blamed or wholly praised.

229. The intelligent examining day by day, praise him who is of flawless life, wise, and endowed with knowledge and virtue.

[1] See note 14 on v. 31.

[2] To a bhikkhu who stands at the door for alms without asking.

[3] Nibbāna. [4] See note 11 on v. 89. [5] Name of a person.

230. Who deigns to blame him who is like refined gold? Even the gods praise him; by Brahmā too is he praised.

231. One should guard against misdeeds (caused by) body, and one should be restrained in body; giving up evil conduct in body, one should be of good bodily conduct.

232. One should guard against misdeeds (caused by) speech, and one should be restrained in speech; giving up evil conduct in speech, one should be of good conduct in speech.

233. One should guard against misdeeds (caused by) mind, and one should be restrained in mind; giving up evil conduct in mind, one should be of good conduct in mind.

234. The wise are restrained in deed; in speech, too they are restrained; they are restrained in mind as well; yea, they are fully restrained.

XVIII. MALAVAGGA. TAINTS

235. Like a withered leaf are you now; the messengers of death wait on you. On the threshold of decay you stand. Provision [1] too there is none for you.

236. Make an island [2] unto yourself; strive quickly; become wise; purged of stain and passionless, you shall enter the heavenly stage [3] of the Ariyas.[4]

237. Your life has come to an end now; to the presence of death you are setting out. No halting place is there for you by the way. Provision too there is none for you.

238. Make an island unto yourself. Strive without delay; fast; become wise. Purged of stain and passionless, you will not come again to birth and old age.[5]

239. By degrees a wise man, little by little, from time to time, should remove his own impurities, as a smith removes (the dross) of silver.

240. As rust sprung from iron, eats itself away when arisen; even so his own deeds lead the transgressor [6] to states of woe.

[1] Provision of merit for the other world.

[2] *Dīpa* is used in the sense of lamp too. Here the term is applied to an island which serves as a place of safety to the shipwrecked.

[3] *Suddhāvāsa* or the Pure Abode where the *Anāgāmis* (Non-Returners) reside.

[4] The Buddha spoke these two verses to an old dying man, when his son performed a meritorious act in his name.

[5] This refers to Arahatship.

[6] *Atidhonacāri*—the bhikkhu who lives without reflecting on the necessaries of life. (Cy.) Whilst using the four necessaries, namely, robes, alms, lodging, and beverages, a bhikkhu is expected to reflect on their special usefulness and on their loathsomeness. If he does not, he transgresses by not using them properly. *Dhona* means the four necessaries.

241. Non-recitation is the rust of doctrines [7]; non-exertion is the rust of homes [8]; sloth is the taint of beauty; carelessness is the flaw of a watcher.

242. Misconduct is the taint of a woman; stinginess is the taint of a donor. Taints, indeed, are all evil things both in this world and in the next.

243. A worse taint than these is Ignorance, the greatest taint. Abandoning this taint be taintless, O bhikkhus!

244. Easy is the life of a shameless one who, with the boldness of a crow, is back-biting, forward, arrogant, and corrupt.

245. Hard is the life of a modest one who ever seeks purity, is detached, humble, clean in life, and reflective.

246, 247. Whoso in this world destroys life; tells lies, takes what is not given, goes to others' wives, and the man who is addicted to intoxicating drinks, such a one digs up his own root [9] in this very world.

248. Know thus, O good man! "Not easy of restraint are evil things." Let not greed and wickedness drag you to protracted misery.

249. People give according to their faith and as they are pleased. Whoever therein is envious of others' food and drink, gains no peace [10] either by day or by night.

250. But he who has this (feeling) fully cut off, uprooted and destroyed, gains peace by day and by night.

251. There is no fire like lust, no grip like hate; there is no net like delusion, no river like craving.

252. Easily seen are others' faults, hard indeed to see are one's

[7] *Manta* means both sciences and religious teachings.

[8] *Ghara* is interpreted as householders.

[9] Of prosperity.

[10] *Samādhi*—mundane or supramundane concentration.

own ; like chaff one winnows others' faults, but one's own one hides, as a crafty fowler covers himself.

253. He who sees others' faults, and is ever irritable, the corruptions of such a one grow. He is far from the destruction of the corruptions.[11]

254. In the sky there is no track. Outside there is no saint.[12] Mankind delights in obstacles.[13] The *Tathāgatas* [14] are free from obstacles.

255. In the sky there is no track. Outside there is no Saint. There is no compound thing that is eternal. There is no instability in the Buddhas.

[11] Namely, the Fruit of Arahatship. See notes on v. 89.

[12] Outside the way. Here Saint refers to one who has realized the four Paths and Fruits.

[13] *Papañca*, namely, craving, pride, and false belief.

[14] Literally, " who has thus come ", or " who has thus gone ". It is an epithet of the Buddha.

XIX. *DHAMMAṬṬHAVAGGA. THE JUST OR THE RIGHTEOUS*

256. He is not thereby 'just' because he hastily [1] arbitrates. The wise man should investigate both right and wrong.[2]

257. The intelligent man who leads others not falsely but lawfully and impartially, and is guarded by the Dhamma, is called " one who stands in the Dhamma (*dhammaṭṭha*) ".

258. He is not thereby a learned man merely because he speaks much ; he who is secure, without hate, and fearless, is called learned.

259. He is not versed in the Dhamma because he speaks much ; he who hears little and sees the Truth mentally [3] is, indeed, versed in the Dhamma, and who is not heedless of the Dhamma.

260. He is not therefore an 'elder' [4] merely because his head is grey ; ripe is he in age, " old-in-vain " is he called.

261. In whom are truth, virtue, harmlessness, restraint, and control, that wise man who has cast out impurities is indeed called an elder.

262. Not by mere eloquence, nor by beautiful appearance does a man become " good-natured ", should he be jealous, selfish, and deceitful.

263. But in whom these are wholly cut off, uprooted, and

[1] *Sahasā*, falsely or unfairly influenced by desire, hatred, fear, and ignorance.

[2] What is true and what is untrue.

[3] *Kāyena*, that is *nāmakāyena*, through the mental body (Cy.), or in other words, through self-realization.

[4] *Thera*, a term applied to those bhikkhus who have counted at least ten years in the Order from the date of their higher ordination.

extinct, that wise man who has cast out hatred is indeed called "good-natured".

264. Not by a shaven head does an undisciplined [5] man, who utters lies, become an ascetic. How will one be an ascetic who is full of desire and greed?

265. He who subdues evil deeds both small and great entirely, because he has overcome all evil deeds, is called an ascetic.

266. He is not therefore a bhikkhu merely because he begs [6] from others; by following ill-smelling actions [7] one certainly does not become a bhikkhu.[8]

267. Herein he who has abandoned both merit and demerit, he who is holy, he who lives with understanding in this world, he indeed is called a bhikkhu.

268. Not by silence (alone) does he become a sage who is dull and ignorant, but he who, as if holding a pair of scales, embraces the best and shuns evil, is indeed a wise man.

269. The sage avoids evils: for that reason he is a sage; he that understands both worlds [9] is therefore called a sage.

270. He is not therefore an Ariya in that he harms living

[5] He who does not practise higher morality (*sīla*) and austerities (*dhutanga*).

[6] Bhikkhus do not beg. They silently stand at the door for alms. See note on v. 224.

[7] *Vissaṃ dhammaṃ.* = *visamaṃ dhammaṃ*; missaṃ gandhaṃ vā kāyakammādikaṃ dhammaṃ. (Cy.)

Vissaṃ has two meanings, whole or all, and bad smell. The commentary gives only the latter in this case.

[8] An alien ascetic who used to beg food approached the Buddha and claimed the right to be called a bhikkhu. Thereupon the Buddha uttered these verses to show that by the mere act of begging one does not become a bhikkhu.

[9] Internal and external aggregates.

beings ; through his harmlessness towards all living beings is he called an Ariya.[10]

271, 272. Not only by mere morality [11] nor again by much learning,[12] nor even by gaining concentration, nor by lonely lodging, (thinking) "I enjoy the bliss of renunciation [13] not resorted to by the worldling", (not with these) should you, O bhikkhu, rest content [14] without reaching the extinction of the corruptions.[15]

[10] This verse was uttered by the Buddha to a fisher named Ariya. See p. xi.

[11] The four kinds of Higher Morality observed by bhikkhus and the thirteen kinds of higher ascetic practices (*dhutanga*). (Cy.)

[12] That is, the Tipiṭaka. (Cy.)

[13] Anāgāmi stage. (Cy.)

[14] Faith in existence. (Cy.) "Have a care", Mrs. Rhys Davids.

[15] That is, Arahatship.

XX. MAGGAVAGGA. THE WAY

273. Of paths the Eightfold [1] is the best, of truths the four Sayings [2] (are the best); dispassion [3] is the best of states and of bipeds the Seeing One.[4]

274. This is the only Way, there is none other for the purity of vision; do you follow this Path. This is the bewilderment of Māra.

275. Entering upon that Path you will make an end of pain; having learnt have I taught you the Path that removes the thorns.[5]

276. You yourselves must make an effort; the Tathāgatas are only teachers. The meditative ones who enter the way are delivered from the bonds of Māra.

277. "Transient are all compound things": when this one discerns with wisdom, then is one disgusted with Ill [6]; this is the Path to Purity.

278. "Sorrowful are all compound things": when this one discerns with wisdom, then is one disgusted with Ill; this is the Path to Purity.

279. "Everything that is,[7] is without self"; when this one

[1] The Eightfold Path consists in: right knowledge, right thoughts, right speech, right action, right livelihood, right effort, right mindfulness, and right concentration.

[2] The four Sayings are the four Noble Truths, Suffering, the Cause of Suffering, the Destruction of Suffering, and the Path leading to the Destruction of Suffering.

[3] *Virāga* = Nibbāna. [4] *Cakkhumā* = the Buddha. [5] Of lust, etc.

[6] Suffering caused by attending to the aggregates.

[7] Impermanence (*anicca*), sorrow (*dukkha*), and selflessness (*anattā*) are the three characteristics of all things conditioned by causes (*sankhārā*). It is

discerns with wisdom, then is one disgusted with Ill; this is the Path to Purity.

280. The idler who strives not when he should strive, who though young and strong is slothful, with mind and purpose depressed, the lazy one does not by wisdom realize the Path.

281. Watchful of speech, well restrained in mind, let him do nought unskilful through his body; let him purify these three ways of action, and win the Path realized by the sages.

282. Indeed from meditation wisdom arises, without meditation wisdom wanes; knowing this twofold path of gain and loss, so let him conduct himself that wisdom grows.

283. Cut down the forest (of passion),[8] but not real trees; from the forest (of passions) springs fear; cutting down both forest and brushwood (of passions), be forestless,[9] O bhikkhus.

284. For as long as the brushwood (of passions) of man towards women is not cut down even a jot, so long is his mind in bondage, like the milch calf to its mother-cow.

285. Cut off your affection as an autumn lily with the hand; cultivate the very path of Peace. Nibbāna has been expounded by the Auspicious One.

by contemplating them that one realizes Nibbāna. The aspirant may choose any characteristic that appeals to him most.

Anattā or selflessness is the crux of Buddhism. The term *samkhāra*, 'compound', which is applied to any conditioned thing, is used in the two previous verses, whilst in the third verse the term *dhamma* is used in order to show that everything, including the unconditioned Nibbāna, is without a soul. Nibbāna is not included in *samkhārā*. It is neither transient nor painful. *Dhamma* embraces both the conditioned and the non-conditioned. Nibbāna is, and is soulless.

[8] When the Buddha said, "Cut down the forest," some newly ordained bhikkhus misconstrued this saying and thought of felling trees. Warning them against such an action the Buddha uttered this.

[9] i.e. passionless.

286. Here will I live in the rains, here in the autumn and the summer: thus the fool muses. He realizes not the danger (of death).

287. The doting man with mind set on children and herds death seizes and carries away, as a great flood a slumbering village.

288. No sons are there to give protection, neither father nor even kinsmen; for him who is overcome by death no protection is to be found among kinsmen.

289. Understanding this fact let the virtuous and wise person swiftly clear the way that leads to Nibbāna.

XXI. PAKIṆṆAKAVAGGA. MISCELLANEOUS

290. If by giving up a slight happiness one may behold a larger one, let the wise person give up the lesser happiness in consideration for the greater happiness.

291. He who wishes his own happiness by causing pain to others is not released from hatred, being himself entangled in the tangles of hatred.

292. What should be done is left undone ; what should not be done is done ; of those who are puffed up and heedless the corruptions increase.

293. They who always practise well " mindfulness of the body ",[1] who follow not what should not be done and constantly do what should be done, of those mindful and reflective ones the corruptions come to an end.

294. Having slain mother (craving) and father (conceit), and two warrior kings (views of eternalism and nihilism), and having destroyed a country (sense-avenues and sense-objects) together with its revenue officer (attachment), ungrieving goes the brāhmaṇa (arahat).

295. Having slain mother and father and two brahmin kings,[2] and having destroyed the perilous path [3] (hindrances), ungrieving goes the brāhmaṇa.

296. Well awakened ever the disciples of Gotama arise ; they

[1] *Kāyagatasati*, contemplation on the loathsomeness of the body.

[2] Views of eternalism and nihilism.

[3] *Veyyagghapañcamaṃ*—this term is used to denote the five hindrances (*nīvaraṇa*) of which doubt or indecision is the fifth. A dangerous and perilous path infested with tigers is called *veyyaggha*. Doubt or indecision is comparable to such a path. (Cy.)

The other four hindrances are sense-desires (*kāmacchanda*), ill-will who by day and by night always contemplate the Buddha.[4]

297. Well awakened ever the disciples of Gotama arise ; they who by day and by night always contemplate the Dhamma.[5]

298. Well awakened ever the disciples of Gotama arise ; they who by day and by night always contemplate the Sangha.[6]

299. Well awakened ever the disciples of Gotama arise ; they who by day and by night always contemplate the body.[7]

300. Well awakened ever the disciples of Gotama arise ; they who by day and by night delight in harmlessness.

301. Well awakened ever the disciples of Gotama arise ; they who by day and by night delight in meditation.

302. Difficult is renunciation, difficult is it to delight therein, difficult and painful is household life, painful is association with unequals ; ill befalls a wayfarer (in *saṃsāra*) ; therefore be not a wayfarer, be not a pursuer of ill.

303. He who is full of confidence [8] and virtue, possessed of repute and wealth, everywhere, in whatever land he sojourns, he is honoured.

304. Even from afar the good reveal themselves like the Himalaya mountain ; the wicked though near are invisible like arrows shot by night.

305. He who sits alone, rests alone, walks alone unwearied, who alone controls oneself, will find delight in the forest.

(*vyāpāda*), restlessness and brooding (*uddhacca-kukkucca*), and sloth and torpor (*thīna-middha*).

They are called hindrances because they obstruct the path to heavenly bliss and Nibbāna. See *A Manual of Buddhism* by the translator.

[4] Reflection on the virtues of the Buddha.

[5] Reflection on the virtues of the Dhamma.

[6] Reflection on the virtues of the Sangha.

[7] Contemplation on the loathsomeness of the body.

[8] *Saddhā*, trustful confidence based on knowledge. There is no blind faith in Buddhism.

XXII. NIRAYAVAGGA. HELL[1]

306. The speaker of untruth goes to hell; and also he who having done it says, "I did not"; both after death become equal, men of base actions in the other world.

307. Many on whose neck is the yellow robe are of evil disposition and uncontrolled; evil ones by their evil deeds are born in hell.

308. Better to eat an iron ball red-hot, like a flame of fire, than as an immoral, uncontrolled person to eat the alms of people.

309. Four misfortunes befall a careless man who commits adultery: acquisition of demerit, disturbed sleep, blame the third, and hell the fourth.

310. There is also acquisition of demerit as well as evil destiny; brief is the joy of the frightened man and woman; the king imposes a heavy punishment; hence no man should frequent another's wife.

311. Just as kusa grass wrongly grasped cuts the hand indeed; even so the ascetic life wrongly handled drags one to hell.

312. Any loose act, any corrupt vow, a dubious holy life, none of this is of great fruit.

313. If aught should be done, let one do it; let one promote it steadily, for slack asceticism scatters dust all the more.

314. An evil deed is better not done; a misdeed hereafter

[1] *Niraya* (lit., devoid of happiness), in whatever life, in whatever world, is not eternal, but ends, for any person, when the evil kamma that produced rebirth is worked out. Neither hell nor heaven, according to Buddhism, is eternal.

torments one ; better it is to do a good deed, after doing which one does not grieve.

315. Like a border city, guarded within and without, so guard yourself ; surely, do not let slip this opportunity, for they who let slip the opportunity [2] grieve when born in hell.

316. Beings who are ashamed of what is not shameful, and are not ashamed of what is shameful, embrace false views and go to a woeful state.

317. Beings who see fear in what is not to be feared, and see no fear in the fearsome, embrace false views and go to a woeful state.

318. Beings who imagine wrong in the faultless [3] and view no wrong in what is wrong,[4] embrace false views and go to a woeful state.

319. Beings knowing wrong as wrong and what is right as right, embrace right views and go to a blissful state.

[2] The birth of the Buddhas, etc.

[3] *Avajja* refers to the ten kinds of right belief.

[4] *Vajja* refers to the ten kinds of wrong belief.

XXIII. NĀGAVAGGA. THE ELEPHANT

320. As an elephant in the battlefield withstands the arrows shot from a bow, even so will I endure abuse ; verily most people are undisciplined.

321. They lead the trained (horses or elephants) to an assembly. The king mounts the trained ; best among men are the trained who endure abuse.

322. Excellent are trained mules, so are thoroughbreds of Sindh and noble elephants, the tuskers ; but far more excellent is he that trains himself.

323. Surely never by those vehicles would one go to the untrodden land (*Nibbāna*), as does one who is controlled through his subdued and well-trained self.

324. The uncontrollable, captive tusker, named Dhanapālaka, with pungent rut flowing, eats no morsel ; the tusker calls to mind the elephant forest.[1]

325. The stupid one, when he is torpid, gluttonous, sleepy, rolls about as he lies like a great hog nourished on pig-wash, again and again goes to rebirth.

326. Formerly this mind went wandering where it liked, as it wished, as it listed ; today with attentiveness I shall completely hold it in check, as a mahout a rut-elephant.

327. Take delight in heedfulness ; guard your mind well. Draw yourself out of the evil way like an elephant sunk in the mire.

328. If you get a prudent companion (who is fit) to live with

[1] The story associated in the commentary with these lines is that of a captive elephant who was supporting its mother in the forest.

you, who behaves well and is wise, you should live with him, joyfully and mindfully overcoming all dangers.

329. If you do not get a prudent companion (who is fit) to live with you, who behaves well, and is wise, then like a king who leaves a conquered kingdom, you should live alone as an elephant in the elephant forest.

330. Better it is to live alone. There is no fellowship with a fool; let one live alone doing no evil, being care-free, like an elephant in the elephant forest.

331. When need arises, happy (is it to have) friends; happy is contentment with just this and that; merit is happy, when life is at an end; happy is the shunning of all ill.

332. Happy in this world is ministering to mother,[2] ministering to father too is happy; happy in this world is ministering to ascetics; happy too is ministering to the Noble Ones.[3]

333. Happy is virtue till old age; happy is steadfast confidence; happy is the attainment of wisdom; happy is it to do no evil.

[2] *Metteyyatā* does not mean motherhood or "to have a mother". The commentarial explanation is good conduct (*sammā-patipatti*) towards the mother, that is, ministering to the mother. The other terms are similarly explained.

[3] Buddha, etc.

XXIV. TAṆHĀVAGGA. CRAVING

334. The craving of the person addicted to careless living grows like a creeper; he jumps from life to life like a fruit-loving monkey in the forest.

335. Whomsoever in this world this base clinging thirst overcomes, his sorrows flourish like well-watered bīraṇa grass.

336. Whoso in the world overcomes this base unruly craving,[1] from him sorrows fall away, like water-drops from a lotus-leaf.

337. This I say to you, Good luck to you all who have assembled here; dig up the root of craving, as one in quest of bīraṇa's sweet root. Let not Māra crush you again and again, as the flood a reed.

338. Just as a tree, with roots undamaged and firm, though hewn down, sprouts again; even so, while latent craving is not rooted out, this sorrow springs up again and again.

339. In whom the thirty-six streams (of craving) that rush towards pleasurable objects[2] are strong, then powerful, lustful thoughts carry off that misunderstanding person.

340. The streams (cravings) flow everywhere. The creeper sprouts and stands; seeing the creeper that has sprung up, with wisdom cut off the root.

[1] Craving is threefold, viz. craving for sensual pleasures (*kāmataṇhā*), craving connected with the view of eternalism (*bhavataṇhā*), and craving connected with the view of nihilism (*vibhavataṇhā*). Craving for personal sense-fields, such as eye, ear, nose, tongue, body, and mind, and for external sense-fields, such as form, sound, scent, taste, contact, and dhammas (objects), when viewed in the above three aspects, divides itself into thirty-six varieties.

[2] Through the six sense-doors.

341. To beings there arise pleasures that rush (towards sense-objects) and are moistened (with craving); bent on pleasure they seek happiness. Verily, those men come to birth and decay.

342. Folk enwrapt in craving are terrified like a captive hare; held fast by fetters and bonds,[3] for long they come to sorrow again and again.

343. Folk enwrapt in craving are terrified like a captive hare; therefore a bhikkhu, who wishes his own passionlessness (Nibbāna), should discard craving.

344. Whoever with no desire (for the household) finds pleasure in the forest (of asceticism), and though freed from desire (for the household), (yet) runs back to that very home, behold that very man! Freed he runs back to that very bondage.[4]

345. That which is made of iron, wood, or hemp is not a strong bond, say the wise; (but) that longing for jewels, ornaments, children, and wives is far greater an attachment.

346. That bond is strong, say the wise, it hurls down, yields, and is hard to loosen; this too they cut off, and leave the world, with no longing renouncing sensual pleasures.

347. They who are infatuated with lust fall back into the stream as a spider on its self-spun web; this too the wise cut off and wander, with no longing, giving up all sorrow.

348. Let go[5] the past, let go the future, let go the present (front, back and middle); crossing to the farther shore of exist-

[3] There are five kinds of bonds (*sangas*), viz. lust, hatred, delusion, pride, and false views.

[4] This verse was uttered apropos a young man who, through faith, entered the Order, but later, tempted by sensual pleasures, returned to the household life.

Here is a pun on the two meanings of *vana*, forest and desire.

[5] That is, attachment to the past, present, and future aggregates.

ence, with mind released from everything, do not again undergo birth and decay.

349. For the person who is perturbed by (evil) thoughts, who is of strong passions, who sees but the pleasurable, craving steadily grows. Indeed, he makes the bond strong.

350. He who delights in subduing (evil) thoughts, he who meditates on Impurity,[6] he who is ever mindful, it is he who will make an end (of craving), he will cut Māra's bond.

351. He who has reached the goal, is fearless, is without craving, is passionless, has cut the thorns of life; this is his final body.

352. He who is without craving and grasping, he who is skilled in etymology and terms,[7] he who knows the grouping of letters and their sequence, it is he who is called the bearer of the final body, one of profound wisdom, a great man.

353. All have I overcome, all do I know; from all am I detached, all have I renounced; wholly absorbed am I in the "Destruction of Craving".[8] Having comprehended all by myself whom shall I call my teacher?[9]

354. The gift of Truth excels all gifts; the flavour of Truth excels all flavours; the pleasure in Truth excels all pleasures; he who has destroyed craving overcomes all sorrow.

355. Riches ruin the foolish, but not those in quest of the

[6] That is, the meditation on the loathsomeness of the body. The chief object of this meditation is to get rid of the attachment to this so-called form.

[7] *Niruttipadakovido*, versed in the four kinds of analytical knowledge (*paṭisambhidā*), viz. meaning (*attha*), text (*dhamma*), etymology (*nirutti*), and understanding (*paṭibhāna*).

[8] *Arahatship*.

[9] This was the Buddha's answer to Upaka, a wandering ascetic, who questioned him about his teacher. Secular teachers the Buddha had before his Enlightenment, but he had none for his Enlightenment.

Beyond (Nibbāna) ; through craving for riches, the foolish one ruins himself as (if he were ruining) others.

356. Weeds are the bane of fields, lust is the bane of this mankind ; hence what is given to the lustless yields abundant fruit.

357. Weeds are the bane of fields, hatred is the bane of this mankind ; hence what is given to those rid of hatred yields abundant fruit.

358. Weeds are the bane of fields, delusion is the bane of this mankind ; hence what is given to those rid of delusion yields abundant fruit.

359. Weeds are the bane of fields, desire is the bane of this mankind ; hence what is given to the desireless yields abundant fruit.

XXV. BHIKKHUVAGGA. THE BHIKKHU OR MENDICANT MONK[1]

360. Good is restraint in the eye; good is restraint in the ear; good is restraint in the nose; good is restraint in the tongue.

361. Good is restraint in deed; good is restraint in speech; good is restraint in mind; good is restraint in everything.[2] The bhikkhu restrained everywhere is freed from all sorrow.

362. He who is controlled in hand, foot, speech, and in the highest (head), he who delights in meditation,[3] and is composed, he who is alone and contented, him they call a bhikkhu.

363. That bhikkhu who is controlled in tongue, who speaks wisely,[4] who is not puffed up, who explains the meaning and the text, sweet, indeed, is his speech.

364. That bhikkhu who dwells in the Dhamma, who delights in the Dhamma, who meditates on the Dhamma, who well remembers the Dhamma, does not fall away from the sublime Dhamma.

365. Let him not despise what he has received, nor fare envying (the gains) of others. The bhikkhu who envies (the gains) of others does not attain concentration.[5]

366. Though a recipient of little, if a bhikkhu does not despise what he has received, even the gods praise him who is pure in livelihood and is not slothful.

[1] Bhikkhu is exclusively a Buddhist term. Mendicant monk may be suggested as the best rendering for bhikkhu.

[2] *Sabbattha*, in all senses.

[3] Here *ajjhatta* refers to the subject of meditation.

[4] *Manta* here means wisdom. (Cy.)

[5] *Samādhi*, both mundane and supramundane concentration.

367. He who has no thought of "I and mine" whatever towards mind and body, he who grieves not for that which he has not, he is indeed called a bhikkhu.

368. The bhikkhu who abides in loving-kindness, who is pleased with the Buddha's teaching, attains to that state of peace and happiness, the stilling of conditioned things.

369. Empty this boat,[6] O bhikkhu ! Emptied by you it will move swiftly ; cutting off lust and hatred, to Nibbāna you will thereby go.

370. Five cut off,[7] five give up,[8] five further cultivate.[9] The bhikkhu who has gone beyond the five bonds [10] is called a "Flood-Crosser".

371. Meditate, O bhikkhu ! Be not heedless. Do not let your mind whirl on sensual pleasures. Do not be careless and swallow a lead-ball. As you burn cry not "This is sorrow."

372. There is no concentration to one who lacks wisdom, nor is there wisdom to him who lacks concentration. In whom are both concentration and wisdom, he, indeed, is in the presence of Nibbāna.

373. The bhikkhu who has retired to a lonely abode, who has calmed his mind, who clearly perceives the Doctrine, experiences a joy transcending that of men.

[6] The boat resembles the body, water resembles bad thoughts.

[7] They are the five fetters that pertain to this shore, namely, self-illusion, doubt, indulgence in wrongful rites and ceremonies, sense-desire and hatred (*orambhāgiya-saṃyojana*).

[8] They are the five fetters that pertain to the Further Shore, namely, attachment to the Realm of Form, attachment to the Formless Realms, conceit, restlessness, and ignorance (*uddhambhāgiya-saṃyojana*).

[9] Namely, confidence (*saddhā*), mindfulness (*sati*), effort (*viriya*), concentration (*samādhi*) and wisdom (*paññā*). These five factors have to be cultivated to destroy the fetters.

[10] See v. 342.

374. Whenever he reflects on the rise and fall of the aggregates, he experiences joy and happiness. To the perspicacious ones that (reflection) [11] is Deathless.

375. And this becomes the beginning here for a wise bhikkhu: sense-control, contentment, restraint with regard to the fundamental Moral Code (*Pātimokkha*), association with beneficent and energetic friends whose livelihood is pure.

376. Let him be cordial in his ways and refined in conduct; thereby full of joy he will make an end of ill.

377. As the jasmine creeper sheds its withered flowers, even so, O bhikkhus, should you totally cast off lust and hatred.

378. The bhikkhu who is calm in body, calm in speech, calm in mind, who is well-composed, who has spewed out worldly things, is truly called a "peaceful one".

379. By self do you censure yourself, by self do you examine yourself. Self-guarded and mindful, O bhikkhu, you will live happily.

380. Self, indeed, is the protector of self; self, indeed, is one's refuge; control therefore your own self as a merchant, a noble steed.

381. Full of joy, full of confidence in the Buddha's Teaching, the bhikkhu will attain the Peaceful State, the stilling of conditioned things, the bliss (supreme).

382. The bhikkhu who, while still young, devotes himself to the Buddha's teaching, illumines this world like the moon freed from a cloud.

[11] As it leads to Nibbāna.

XXVI. BRĀHMAṆAVAGGA. THE BRĀHMAṆA[1]

383. Strive and cleave the stream; discard, O brāhmaṇa, sense-desires, knowing the destruction of life's constituents, thou art, O brāhmaṇa, a knower of the Uncreate (Nibbāna).

384. When in two states,[2] a brāhmaṇa goes to the farther shore, then all the fetters of that knowing one pass away.

385. For whom there exists neither the hither [3] nor the farther shore,[4] nor both the hither and the farther shore,[5] he who is undistressed and unbound, him I call a brāhmaṇa.

386. He that is meditative, stainless, and settled; he that has done his duty and is free from the Corruptions; he that has attained the Highest Goal, him I call a brāhmaṇa.

387. The sun shines by day, the moon is bright by night; armoured shines the warrior, meditating the brāhmaṇa shines; but all day and night the Buddha [6] shines in glory.

388. Because he has discarded evil, he is called a "*brāhmaṇa*"; because he lives in quietude,[7] he is called a "*samaṇa*"; because he gives up the impurities, he is called a "*pabbajita*" (recluse).

389. One should not strike a brāhmaṇa; a brāhmaṇa should

[1] Though a racial term here it is applied either to a Buddha or to an Arahat, to one who has completed the Way and has won Enlightenment.

[2] Concentration and insight.

[3] The internal six senses.

[4] The external six senses.

[5] An arahat does not view both external and internal senses as "I" or "mine".

[6] The Buddha outshines immorality by the power of morality, vice by the power of virtue, ignorance by the power of wisdom, demerit by the power of merit, unrighteousness by the power of righteousness.

[7] Having subdued all evil.

not vent (his wrath) on him. Shame on him who strikes a brāhmaṇa! More shame on him who gives vent (to his wrath).

390. Unto a brāhmaṇa that (non-retaliation) is of no small advantage. When the mind is weaned from things dear, whenever the intent to harm ceases, then and then only sorrow subsides.

391. He that does no evil through body, speech, or mind, who is restrained in these three respects, him I call a brāhmaṇa.

392. If from anybody one should understand the Doctrine preached by the Fully Enlightened One, devoutly should one reverence him, as a brāhmaṇa reveres the sacrificial fire.

393. Not by matted hair, nor by family, nor by birth does one become a brāhmaṇa; but in whom there exist both truth[8] and righteousness,[9] pure is he, a brāhmaṇa is he.

394. What is the use of your matted hair, O witless man! What is the use of your antelope garment? Within you are full (of passions), without you embellish.[10]

395. The person who wears dust-heap robes,[11] who is lean, who is overspread with veins, who meditates alone in the forest, him I call a brāhmaṇa.

396. I do not call him a brāhmaṇa merely because he is born of a womb or sprung from a brāhmaṇa mother. He is merely a "Dear addresser",[12] if he is with impediments. He who is free from impediments, free from clinging, him I call a brāhmaṇa.

[8] The realization of the four Noble Truths.

[9] Here Dhamma refers to the nine Supramundane States.

[10] With the paraphernalia of the ascetics.

[11] Robes made of cast-off pieces of cloth.

[12] *Bho* is a familiar form of address which even the Buddha uses to laymen. The term *bhovādi* is applied to the Buddha as well.

397. He who has cut off all fetters, who trembles not, who has gone beyond ties, who is unbound, him I call a brāhmaṇa.

398. He who has cut the strap (hatred), the thong (craving), and the rope (heresies), together with the appendages (latent tendencies), who has thrown up the cross-bar (ignorance), who is enlightened (buddha), him I call a brāhmaṇa.

399. He who, without anger, endures reproach, flogging and punishments, whose power, the potent army, is patience, him I call a brāhmaṇa.

400. He who is not wrathful, but is dutiful, virtuous, not moistened with craving, controlled, and bears his final body, him I call a brāhmaṇa.

401. Like water on a lotus leaf, like a mustard seed on the point of a needle, he clings not to sensual pleasures, him I call a brāhmaṇa.

402. He who realizes here in this world the destruction of his sorrow, who has laid the burden aside and is emancipated, him I call a brāhmaṇa.

403. He whose knowledge is deep, who is wise, who is skilled in the right and wrong way, who has reached the highest goal, him I call a brāhmaṇa.

404. He who is not intimate with both householders and homeless ones, who wanders without an abode, who is without desires, him I call a brāhmaṇa.

405. He who has laid aside the cudgel towards beings, whether feeble or strong, who neither kills nor causes to kill, him I call a brāhmaṇa.

406. He who is friendly amongst the hostile, who is peaceful amongst the violent, who is unattached amongst the attached,[13] him I call a brāhmaṇa.

407. In whom lust, hatred, pride, detraction are fallen off like

[13] Those who are attached to the aggregates.

a mustard seed from the point of a needle, him I call a brāhmaṇa.

408. He who utters gentle, instructive, true words, who gives offence to none, him I call a brāhmaṇa.

409. He who in this world takes nothing that is not given, be it long or short, small or great, fair or foul, him I call a brāhmaṇa.

410. He who has no desires, whether of this world or of the next, who is desireless and emancipated, him I call a brāhmaṇa.

411. He who has no longings, who through knowledge is free from doubts, who has plunged into the Deathless (Nibbāna), him I call a brāhmaṇa.

412. Herein he who has transcended both good and bad and the ties as well, who is sorrowless, stainless, and pure, him I call a brāhmaṇa.

413. He who is spotless as the moon, who is pure, serene, and still, who has destroyed craving for becoming,[14] him I call a brāhmaṇa.

414. He who has passed beyond this quagmire, this difficult path, the ocean of life (saṃsāra), and delusion, who has crossed and gone beyond, who is meditative, free from craving and doubts, who, clinging to nought, has attained Nibbāna, him I call a brāhmaṇa.

415. He who in this world giving up sensual pleasures, would renounce and become a homeless one, who has destroyed sense-desires and becoming, him I call a brāhmaṇa.

416. He who in this world giving up craving, would renounce and become a homeless one, who has destroyed craving and becoming, him I call a brāhmaṇa.

417. He who, discarding human ties and transcending celestial ties, is completely delivered from all ties, him I call a brāhmaṇa.

[14] *Bhava*, the threefold existence, the sentient realm, the Realm of Form, and the Formless Realm.

418. He who has given up likes and dislikes, who is cooled and is without substrata,[15] who has conquered the world, and is strenuous, him I call a brāhmaṇa.

419. He who, in every way, knows the death and rebirth of beings, who is detached,[16] well-gone,[17] and enlightened, him I call a brāhmaṇa.

420. He whose destiny neither gods nor gandhabbas[18] nor men know, who has destroyed all Defilements, and is an arahat, him I call a brāhmaṇa.

421. He who has no clinging to aggregates that are past, future, or present, who is without clinging and grasping, him I call a brāhmaṇa.

422. The fearless, the noble, the hero, the great sage, the conqueror, the desireless, the enlightened, him I call a brāhmaṇa.

423. That sage who knows his former abodes, who sees heaven and hell, who has reached the end of births, who, with superior wisdom,[19] has perfected himself, who has completed (the holy life) the end of all (passions), him I call a brāhmaṇa.

[15] *Upadhi*—there are four kinds of *upadhi*, namely, the aggregates (*khandha*), the passions (*kilesa*), volitional activities (*abhisaṃkhārā*), and sense-desires (*kāma*).

[16] That is, he who has put an end to the arising of the aggregates.

[17] *Sugata*, gone to Nibbāna.

[18] A class of celestial beings.

[19] Pertaining to the Arahat Path.